Knowing Mathematics

Authors

Dr. Liping Ma
Dr. Cathy Kessel

Blue Level

 HOUGHTON MIFFLIN   BOSTON

ISBN 0-618-24832-3

3 4 5 6 7 8 9 10-HS-11 10 09 08 07 06 05 04

Table of Contents

Meet the Class

Ms. Park loves teaching math. Her students are Danny, Lily, C.J., and Ana, and they like to discuss math with Ms. Park. She always listens to them and helps them build their ideas about math!

Mr. K9 and his son Chip aren't part of the class, but they pay attention to what is happening. Read their comments to get some help in building your own ideas about math!

1-1   What is a number?

Mathematical Conversation

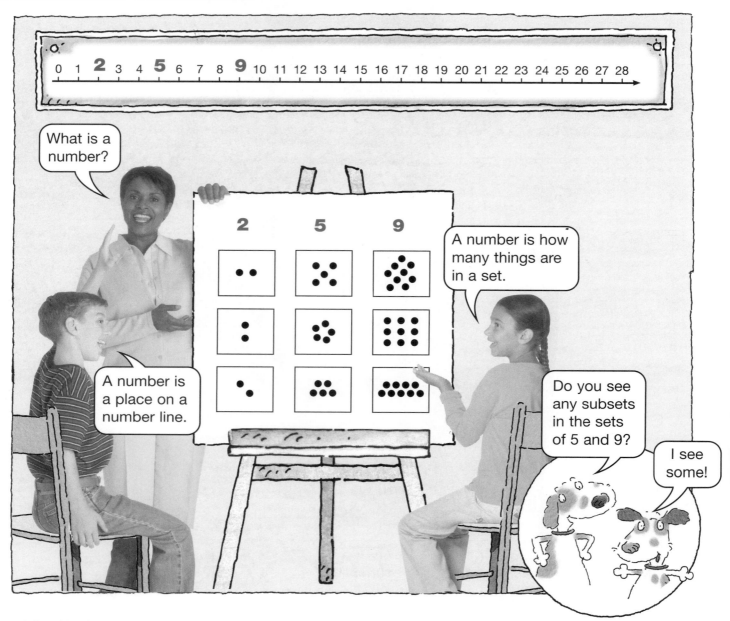

Guided Practice

Circle the subsets that make up each group of dots. Write the number of dots in each set.

A.

5

B.

____

C.

____

D.

____

E.

____

Lesson 1–1 Exercises

Write the number of dots in each set. Try to do it without counting the dots one by one. Circle subsets if it helps.

1.	2.	3.	4.	5.	6.	7.	8.
9.	10.	11.	12.	13.	14.	15.	16.
17.	18.	19.	20.	21.	22.	23.	24.
25.	26.	27.	28.	29.	30.	31.	32.
33.	34.	35.	36.	37.	38.	39.	40.

Word Problems

Write a mathematical expression to represent each problem.
Then calculate and answer the questions.

41. Oscar has 3 green balloons and 3 red balloons. How many balloons does he have in all?

_____

42. Mary has 2 pink balls and 5 purple balls. How many balls does she have altogether?

_____

43. Juan has 8 pens. He gives Tom 3 of them. How many pens does Juan have now?

_____

44. Ping has 9 stamps. Mary has 7 stamps. How many more stamps does Ping have than Mary?

_____

Reflection and Discussion Look for two subsets in this set of dots and circle them. Which dots did you circle? How many dots are in each subset?

1-2 Why is number 10 so special?

Mathematical Conversation

Look at our new "Stand-out Ten" number-line poster.

Wait a minute. On this poster, 10 stands out, but 20, 30, 40 . . . stand out, too. What do numbers like 20, 30, 40 . . . have to do with 10?

Don't you see that 20, 30, 40 . . . are all multiples of 10. 20 has two names. My friend says that "twenty" is its nickname, and "two tens" is its real name. And 30, 40, 50, 60 . . . all have two names, just as 20 does!

What's special about 10? Why don't the multiples of 3, 4, or 5 stand out?

You know what? I think 10 is a special organizer of numbers. See, 10 ones make a 10, 10 tens make a 100, 10 hundreds make a 1,000.

Good for you, Ana! This pattern works for decimals, too. 10 tenths make a 1.

10 is special!

Guided Practice

Write an expression to represent how each set of dots composes a 10.

A.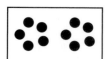

$5 + 5 = 10$

B.

$9 + 1 = 10$

C.

$7 + 3 = 10$

D.

_____

E.

_____

4

Lesson 1–2 Exercises

Fill in the answers. Calculate without using your fingers.

1. $9 + \underline{\hspace{1cm}} = 10$ 2. $8 + \underline{\hspace{1cm}} = 10$ 3. $7 + \underline{\hspace{1cm}} = 10$ 4. $6 + \underline{\hspace{1cm}} = 10$

5. $1 + \underline{\hspace{1cm}} = 10$ 6. $2 + \underline{\hspace{1cm}} = 10$ 7. $3 + \underline{\hspace{1cm}} = 10$ 8. $4 + \underline{\hspace{1cm}} = 10$

9. $10 - \underline{\hspace{1cm}} = 5$ 10. $10 - \underline{\hspace{1cm}} = 9$ 11. $10 - \underline{\hspace{1cm}} = 6$ 12. $10 - \underline{\hspace{1cm}} = 7$

13. $10 - \underline{\hspace{1cm}} = 2$ 14. $10 - \underline{\hspace{1cm}} = 1$ 15. $10 - \underline{\hspace{1cm}} = 3$ 16. $10 - \underline{\hspace{1cm}} = 8$

17. $5 + 5 = \underline{\hspace{1cm}}$ 18. $4 + 5 = \underline{\hspace{1cm}}$ 19. $6 + 4 = \underline{\hspace{1cm}}$ 20. $7 + 3 = \underline{\hspace{1cm}}$

21. $4 + 4 = \underline{\hspace{1cm}}$ 22. $2 + 5 = \underline{\hspace{1cm}}$ 23. $3 + 4 = \underline{\hspace{1cm}}$ 24. $3 + 3 = \underline{\hspace{1cm}}$

25. $10 - 5 = \underline{\hspace{1cm}}$ 26. $8 - 5 = \underline{\hspace{1cm}}$ 27. $10 - 4 = \underline{\hspace{1cm}}$ 28. $10 - 3 = \underline{\hspace{1cm}}$

29. $9 - 4 = \underline{\hspace{1cm}}$ 30. $7 - 5 = \underline{\hspace{1cm}}$ 31. $8 - 5 = \underline{\hspace{1cm}}$ 32. $9 - 6 = \underline{\hspace{1cm}}$

33. $8 + 1 = \underline{\hspace{1cm}}$ 34. $7 - 4 = \underline{\hspace{1cm}}$ 35. $8 - 2 = \underline{\hspace{1cm}}$ 36. $9 + 1 = \underline{\hspace{1cm}}$

37. $6 - 5 = \underline{\hspace{1cm}}$ 38. $10 - 6 = \underline{\hspace{1cm}}$ 39. $4 + 2 = \underline{\hspace{1cm}}$ 40. $2 + 7 = \underline{\hspace{1cm}}$

Write a number to complete each sentence.

41. Three tens make _____.

42. Five tens make _____.

43. Nine tens make _____.

44. Ten tens make _____.

45. Three plus seven is _____.

46. Ten minus seven is _____.

47. Six plus four is _____.

48. Ten minus six is _____.

Reflection and Discussion

How many tens are there in 110?

1-3   Can you turn addition into subtraction?

Mathematical Conversation

Guided Practice

In each box, write three other versions of the equation.

A.	B.	C.	D.	E.	F.
4 + 3 = 7	8 + 2 = 10	5 + 4 = 9	7 + 3 = 10	5 + 3 = 8	4 + 2 = 6
3 + 4 = 7	_____	_____	_____	_____	_____
7 − 3 = 4	_____	_____	_____	_____	_____
7 − 4 = 3	_____	_____	_____	_____	_____

Lesson 1–3 Exercises

In each box, write two addition and two subtraction equations that represent the number and organization of the dots.

1.	2.	3.	4.	5.

6.	7.	8.	9.	10.

11.	12.	13.	14.	15.

(Hint: you can write a multistep equation for 15.)

Fill in the answers. Calculate without using your fingers.

16. Since $4 + 5 = 9$, then $9 - 5 =$ _____ and $9 - 4 =$ _____.

17. Since $2 + 6 = 8$, then $8 - 2 =$ _____ and $8 - 6 =$ _____.

18. Since $1 + 5 = 6$, then $6 - 5 =$ _____ and $6 - 1 =$ _____.

19. Since $10 - 7 = 3$, then $10 - 3 =$ _____ and $3 + 7 =$ _____.

20. Since $9 - 6 = 3$, then $9 - 3 =$ _____ and $3 + 6 =$ _____.

Reflection and Discussion

Can you find other versions for subtraction equations, such as $8 - 2 = 6$?

1-4   Why do we call it "difference"?

Mathematical Conversation

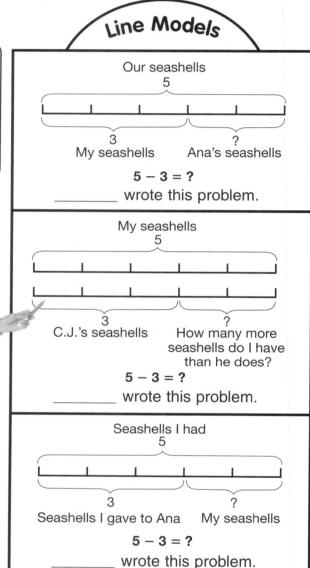

These are line models for word problems that we made up about our seashell collections. Can you tell what the word problems are and who wrote each one?

Line Models

Our seashells
5

3
My seashells

?
Ana's seashells

5 − 3 = ?
_____ wrote this problem.

My seashells
5

3
C.J.'s seashells

?
How many more seashells do I have than he does?

5 − 3 = ?
_____ wrote this problem.

Seashells I had
5

3
Seashells I gave to Ana

?
My seashells

5 − 3 = ?
_____ wrote this problem.

People call the result of addition "sum," and the result of subtraction "difference." Please tell me: what difference is each word problem looking for?

This is the pattern: all of the models of 5 − 3 = ? are about finding the difference between 5 and 3.

I see it!

Guided Practice

Create three different word problems that are represented by this equation.
Use the same topic for all three problems.

7 − 4 = 3

A. _____

B. _____

C. _____

Lesson 1–4 Exercises

Create three different word problems that could be represented by each of these equations. Use the same topic for all three problems.

1.

$10 - 6 = 4$

2.

$8 - 3 = 5$

Draw a line model to represent each of the following expressions.

3. $5 - 3 = $ _____   **4.** $6 - 4 = $ _____   **5.** $4 - 1 = $ _____   **6.** $3 - 2 = $ _____

7. $1 + 3 = $ _____   **8.** $3 + 2 = $ _____   **9.** $4 + 2 = $ _____   **10.** $5 + 1 = $ _____

Write an equation for each problem.

11. What is the sum of 8 and 2? _____

12. What is the sum of 3 and 4? _____

13. What is the difference between 7 and 2? _____

14. What is the difference between 6 and 10? _____

15. How many more than 7 is 10? _____

16. How many is 7 less than 10? _____

Reflection and Discussion We sometimes use line models to represent the difference between two numbers. Do we always use one line? Could we use two lines? How?

1-5   Review, Reflection, and Quiz 1

Mathematical Conversation

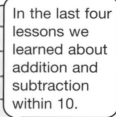

In the last four lessons we learned about addition and subtraction within 10.

But now I can do some addition and subtraction even beyond 10. Since 2 + 3 = 5, then I know that 20 + 30 = 50. Since 4 + 4 = 8, then I know that 40 + 40 = 80!

Cool! Since 20 is 2 tens, and 30 equals 3 tens, then 2 tens plus 3 tens equals 5 tens, 50! Since 40 is 4 tens, then 4 tens plus 4 tens equals 8 tens, 80!

Clever, huh?

I have a cool idea, too. Try this: Can you tell me right away what 7 + 6 + 4 is?

Um . . . Not really.

It's 17! Look, we know that 6 + 4 = 10, and that addends can trade places. So I composed 10 first, then added 7 to it. The answer is 17!

We can always learn new things by reflecting on what we've learned. Try the problems below.

Guided Practice

A. 40 + 30 = _____

B. 80 + 10 = _____

C. 60 + 40 = _____

D. 4 + 8 + 2 = _____

E. 7 + 7 + 3 = _____

F. 8 + 6 + 4 = _____

Quiz 1

Calculate without using your fingers and fill in the answers.

1. 2 + 2 = _____   2. 3 + 2 = _____   3. 4 + 4 = _____   4. 4 + 3 = _____   5. 5 + 5 = _____

6. 5 − 3 = _____   7. 4 − 2 = _____   8. 6 − 3 = _____   9. 7 − 5 = _____   10. 4 − 2 = _____

11. 5 + 2 = _____   12. 6 + 3 = _____   13. 7 + 1 = _____   14. 5 + 4 = _____   15. 7 + 3 = _____

16. 7 − 3 = _____   17. 9 − 2 = _____   18. 8 − 4 = _____   19. 5 − 4 = _____   20. 7 − 6 = _____

21. 5 + _____ = 10   22. 6 + _____ = 10   23. 7 + _____ = 10   24. 4 + _____ = 10

25. 8 + _____ = 10   26. 10 − _____ = 6   27. 10 − _____ = 5   28. 10 − _____ = 1

Calculate the answers. Then write three other versions of each equation.

29.	30.	31.	32.	33.
5 + 3 = ___	4 + 2 = ___	7 + 2 = ___	9 − 3 = ___	7 − 2 = ___
_____	_____	_____	_____	_____
_____	_____	_____	_____	_____
_____	_____	_____	_____	_____

Word Problem

Draw a line model and write a mathematical expression to represent this word problem. Then calculate and answer the question.

34. Mary saw 5 birds in her yard when she got up. While she was having breakfast, 2 more birds arrived. How many birds are in the yard now? _____

    Line Model:

    Mathematical expression:

Challenge Yourself

35. 20 + 20 = _____   36. 30 + 30 = _____   37. 40 + 40 = _____   38. 40 + 30 = _____

39. 50 + 30 = _____   40. 5 + 8 + 2 = _____   41. 9 + 9 + 1 = _____   42. 6 + 7 + 3 = _____

1-6   What is the real name for "eleven"?

Mathematical Conversation

Ana mentioned before that 20, 30, 40 . . . have both real names and nicknames. Did you know that 11 also has two names?

I know! The nickname for 11 is "eleven." Its real name is "ten-and-one"!

Do you mean that all the numbers between 10 and 20 have two names? So the nickname for 12 is "twelve," and its real name is "ten-and-two"?

Yes! The nickname for 13 is "thirteen," and its real name is "ten-and-three"!

The real names for these numbers can help us make sense of them. Do you agree?

Here we see again that 10 is a special organizer of numbers!

Good for you!

Guided Practice

Write the "real names" for the numbers from 11 to 19.

A. Eleven _____   **B.** Twelve _____   **C.** Thirteen _____

D. Fourteen _____   **E.** Fifteen _____   **F.** Sixteen _____

G. Seventeen _____   **H.** Eighteen _____   **I.** Nineteen _____

Lesson 1–6 Exercises

Calculate without using your fingers and fill in the answers.

1. $10 + 5 =$ ____
2. $10 + 2 =$ ____
3. $10 + 4 =$ ____
4. $10 + 8 =$ ____

5. $5 + 10 =$ ____
6. $2 + 10 =$ ____
7. $4 + 10 =$ ____
8. $8 + 10 =$ ____

9. $15 - 5 =$ ____
10. $12 - 2 =$ ____
11. $14 - 4 =$ ____
12. $18 - 8 =$ ____

13. $15 - 10 =$ ____
14. $12 - 10 =$ ____
15. $14 - 10 =$ ____
16. $18 - 10 =$ ____

17. $10 + 6 =$ ____
18. $10 + 3 =$ ____
19. $10 + 7 =$ ____
20. $10 + 9 =$ ____

21. $6 + 10 =$ ____
22. $3 + 10 =$ ____
23. $7 + 10 =$ ____
24. $9 + 10 =$ ____

25. $16 - 6 =$ ____
26. $13 - 3 =$ ____
27. $17 - 7 =$ ____
28. $19 - 9 =$ ____

29. $16 - 10 =$ ____
30. $13 - 10 =$ ____
31. $17 - 10 =$ ____
32. $19 - 10 =$ ____

33. $10 - 8 =$ ____
34. $8 - 2 =$ ____
35. $7 - 4 =$ ____
36. $9 - 3 =$ ____

37. $9 - 5 =$ ____
38. $7 - 2 =$ ____
39. $5 - 4 =$ ____
40. $9 - 6 =$ ____

41. $8 + \underline{5 + 5} =$ ____
42. $9 + \underline{8 + 2} =$ ____
43. $\underline{4 + 6} + 6 =$ ____
44. $\underline{7 + 3} + 4 =$ ____

45. $9 + \underline{9 + 1} =$ ____
46. $6 + \underline{7 + 3} =$ ____
47. $10 - 2 - 3 =$ ____
48. $10 - 8 - 1 =$ ____

Word Problems

Compare the two models. Write a mathematical expression to represent each problem. Then calculate and answer the questions.

49. I have 10 schoolbooks and 3 comic books. How many books is that?

    _____

    Line model:

    Bar model:

    Mathematical expression:

50. I had 18 magazines. I gave away 8 of them. How many magazines do I have now? _____

    Line model:

    Bar model:

    Mathematical expression:

Reflection and Discussion
The nicknames of each teen number provide at least one hint of their real names with one exception. Do you know what these hints are? And what is the exception?

1-7 Do you know the trick for computing with 9?

Mathematical Conversation

Look, I've made an interesting list. Do you see the pattern? Can you fill in the blanks?

I made a list to go with Ana's list. Do you see the pattern? Can you complete my list?

9 + 1 = 10
9 + 2 = 11
9 + 3 = 12
9 + 4 = 13
9 + 5 = 14
9 + 6 = _____
9 + 7 = _____
9 + 8 = _____
9 + 9 = _____

Ana's List	My List
9 + 1 = 10	10 − 9 = 1
9 + 2 = 11	11 − 9 = 2
9 + 3 = 12	12 − 9 = 3
9 + 4 = 13	13 − 9 = 4
9 + 5 = 14	14 − 9 = 5
9 + 6 = 15	15 − 9 = _____
9 + 7 = 16	16 − 9 = _____
9 + 8 = 17	17 − 9 = _____
9 + 9 = 18	18 − 9 = _____

Here's another list that goes with Ana's list. Can you complete this one?

Ana's List	My List
9 + 1 = 10	1 + 9 = _____
9 + 2 = 11	2 + 9 = _____
9 + 3 = 12	3 + 9 = _____
9 + 4 = 13	4 + 9 = _____
9 + 5 = 14	5 + 9 = _____
9 + 6 = 15	6 + 9 = _____
9 + 7 = 16	7 + 9 = _____
9 + 8 = 17	8 + 9 = _____
9 + 9 = 18	9 + 9 = _____

So, what is the trick for computing with 9, and why does it work?

The number 1 seems to play a big role!

Guided Practice

Use the patterns that you found to figure out the sum of each pair of numbers. Memorize each sum.

A.
11	
9	2

B.
9	3

C.
9	4

D.
9	5

E.
9	6

F.
9	7

G.
9	8

H.
9	9

14

Lesson 1–7 Exercises

Calculate without using your fingers and fill in the answers.

1. $9 + 5 =$ _____
2. $9 + 2 =$ _____
3. $9 + 4 =$ _____
4. $9 + 8 =$ _____

5. $9 + 9 =$ _____
6. $9 + 3 =$ _____
7. $9 + 7 =$ _____
8. $9 + 6 =$ _____

9. $2 + 9 =$ _____
10. $5 + 9 =$ _____
11. $4 + 9 =$ _____
12. $3 + 9 =$ _____

13. $6 + 9 =$ _____
14. $0 + 9 =$ _____
15. $8 + 9 =$ _____
16. $7 + 9 =$ _____

17. $11 - 9 =$ _____
18. $18 - 9 =$ _____
19. $13 - 9 =$ _____
20. $14 - 9 =$ _____

21. $15 - 9 =$ _____
22. $16 - 9 =$ _____
23. $17 - 9 =$ _____
24. $12 - 9 =$ _____

25. $13 - 4 =$ _____
26. $14 - 6 =$ _____
27. $17 - 7 =$ _____
28. $17 - 8 =$ _____

29. $12 - 3 =$ _____
30. $11 - 2 =$ _____
31. $15 - 6 =$ _____
32. $18 - 9 =$ _____

33. $13 - 2 =$ _____
34. $18 - 7 =$ _____
35. $17 - 1 =$ _____
36. $16 - 3 =$ _____

37. $9 - 4 =$ _____
38. $15 - 5 =$ _____
39. $18 - 10 =$ _____
40. $17 - 6 =$ _____

41. $8 + 5 - 5 =$ _____
42. $9 + 2 + 8 =$ _____
43. $14 + 6 - 5 =$ _____
44. $17 + 2 - 1 =$ _____

45. $9 + 9 - 8 =$ _____
46. $6 + 5 + 5 =$ _____
47. $12 - 9 - 3 =$ _____
48. $14 - 9 - 2 =$ _____

Word Problems

Compare the models. Write a mathematical expression to represent each problem.
Then calculate and answer the questions.

49. Ms. Park has 19 students in her class. There are 9 boys. How many girls are in her class? _____

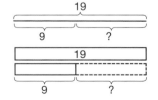

Mathematical expression:

50. Mary has 9 books. Sam has 7 books. How many books do they have altogether? _____

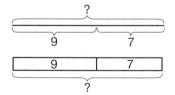

Mathematical expression:

Reflection and Discussion

Can you explain the trick for computing with 9?

1-8   Will computing with 8 be easier?

Mathematical Conversation

Are there any tricks for computing with 8? Can we revise the trick for 9 to make it work for 8?

You know what? I think the number 2 will be important.

8 + 3 = ?

I've got it! Here are the lists. Help me complete them. Don't forget to figure out the pattern.

Hey! The lists for 8 are shorter than the lists for 9.

Unfortunately, "shorter" does not always mean "easier."

Really?

8 + 2 = 10   2 + 8 = _____   10 − 8 = _____
8 + 3 = 11   3 + 8 = _____   11 − 8 = _____
8 + 4 = 12   4 + 8 = _____   12 − 8 = _____
8 + 5 = 13   5 + 8 = _____   13 − 8 = _____
8 + 6 = 14   6 + 8 = _____   14 − 8 = _____
8 + 7 = 15   7 + 8 = _____   15 − 8 = _____
8 + 8 = 16   16 − 8 = _____

Guided Practice

Figure out the sum of each pair of numbers. Memorize each sum.

A.		B.		C.		D.		E.		F.	
11											
8	3	8	4	8	5	8	6	8	7	8	8

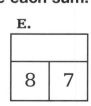

Lesson 1–8 Exercises

Calculate without using your fingers and fill in the answers.

1. $8 + 4 =$ _____   2. $8 + 3 =$ _____   3. $8 + 5 =$ _____   4. $8 + 8 =$ _____

5. $8 + 9 =$ _____   6. $8 + 2 =$ _____   7. $8 + 7 =$ _____   8. $8 + 6 =$ _____

9. $3 + 8 =$ _____   10. $6 + 8 =$ _____   11. $5 + 8 =$ _____   12. $2 + 8 =$ _____

13. $4 + 8 =$ _____   14. $0 + 8 =$ _____   15. $7 + 8 =$ _____   16. $8 + 8 =$ _____

17. $11 - 8 =$ _____   18. $18 - 8 =$ _____   19. $13 - 8 =$ _____   20. $14 - 8 =$ _____

21. $15 - 8 =$ _____   22. $16 - 8 =$ _____   23. $17 - 8 =$ _____   24. $12 - 8 =$ _____

25. $13 - 5 =$ _____   26. $14 - 6 =$ _____   27. $14 - 8 =$ _____   28. $17 - 9 =$ _____

29. $12 - 4 =$ _____   30. $11 - 3 =$ _____   31. $15 - 7 =$ _____   32. $18 - 10 =$ _____

33. $13 + 5 =$ _____   34. $12 + 7 =$ _____   35. $15 + 2 =$ _____   36. $14 + 4 =$ _____

37. $18 - 2 =$ _____   38. $15 - 1 =$ _____   39. $19 - 10 =$ _____   40. $17 - 1 =$ _____

41. $8 + 7 + 3 =$ _____   42. $9 + 4 + 6 =$ _____   43. $14 + 6 - 5 =$ _____   44. $17 + 2 - 1 =$ _____

45. $8 + 9 - 9 =$ _____   46. $2 + 5 + 8 =$ _____   47. $10 - 7 - 3 =$ _____   48. $16 - 2 - 2 =$ _____

Word Problems

Compare the models. Write a mathematical expression to represent each problem.
Then calculate and answer the questions.

49. Tom ate 6 apricots on Monday and 8 on Tuesday. How many apricots did he eat during those two days?

_____

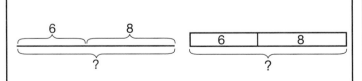

Mathematical expression:

50. There are 14 red cups and 6 white cups. How many more red cups than white cups are there?

_____

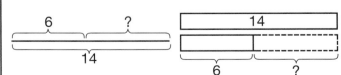

Mathematical expression:

Reflection and Discussion

Do you think that computing with 8 is easier than computing with 9? Why?

1-9   What are the equation lists for 7?

Mathematical Conversation

I guess today we will work on equation lists for 7.

I guess the lists for 7 will be even shorter than for 8.

For 7, you are going to complete all the lists by yourselves.

7 + 3 = _____   3 + 7 = _____   10 − 7 = _____

7 + 4 = _____   4 + 7 = _____   11 − 7 = _____

7 + 5 = _____   5 + 7 = _____   12 − 7 = _____

7 + 6 = _____   6 + 7 = _____   13 − 7 = _____

7 + 7 = _____   14 − 7 = _____

I bet that tomorrow we will work on 6. Why don't we work on the equation list at home and bring it to school? It will be fun to see if we make the same list.

Good idea. Let's do it.

Do you know why 7 + 8 and 7 + 9 are not in the list?

Guided Practice

Figure out the sum of each pair of numbers. Memorize each sum.

A.
7	4

B.
7	5

C.
7	6

D.
7	7

Lesson 1–9 Exercises

Calculate without using your fingers and fill in the answers.

1. $7 + 3 =$ _____

2. $7 + 4 =$ _____

3. $7 + 5 =$ _____

4. $7 + 6 =$ _____

5. $7 + 7 =$ _____

6. $7 + 1 =$ _____

7. $7 + 2 =$ _____

8. $7 + 0 =$ _____

9. $3 + 7 =$ _____

10. $6 + 7 =$ _____

11. $5 + 7 =$ _____

12. $2 + 7 =$ _____

13. $4 + 7 =$ _____

14. $0 + 7 =$ _____

15. $1 + 7 =$ _____

16. $8 + 7 =$ _____

17. $11 - 7 =$ _____

18. $13 - 7 =$ _____

19. $12 - 7 =$ _____

20. $14 - 7 =$ _____

21. $15 - 7 =$ _____

22. $16 - 7 =$ _____

23. $17 - 7 =$ _____

24. $10 - 7 =$ _____

25. $13 - 9 =$ _____

26. $14 - 9 =$ _____

27. $14 - 5 =$ _____

28. $17 - 9 =$ _____

29. $12 - 3 =$ _____

30. $11 - 4 =$ _____

31. $15 - 8 =$ _____

32. $18 - 8 =$ _____

33. $13 + 7 =$ _____

34. $10 + 5 =$ _____

35. $15 + 2 =$ _____

36. $12 + 4 =$ _____

37. $19 - 8 =$ _____

38. $15 - 6 =$ _____

39. $19 - 3 =$ _____

40. $17 - 6 =$ _____

41. $7 + 7 + 1 =$ _____

42. $9 + 7 + 2 =$ _____

43. $11 + 5 - 5 =$ _____

44. $14 + 2 - 2 =$ _____

45. $8 + 7 - 9 =$ _____

46. $3 + 5 + 8 =$ _____

47. $10 - 4 + 3 =$ _____

48. $14 - 2 - 2 =$ _____

Word Problems

Compare the models. Write a mathematical expression to represent each problem. Then calculate and answer the questions.

49. Oscar has 7 computer games. His older brother has 9. How many games do Oscar and his brother have in all? _____

Mathematical expression: _____

50. Mary collected 11 scenic postcards and 4 animal postcards. How many more scenic cards than animal cards did Mary collect? _____

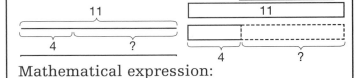

Mathematical expression: _____

Reflection and Discussion

Can you explain why $6 + 7 = 13$, using the idea of 10 as an organizer?

1-10   Review, Reflection, and Quiz 2

Mathematical Conversation

Here's my list for 6.

You forgot these versions.

Ana's List

6 + 4 = _____   10 − 6 = _____
6 + 5 = _____   11 − 6 = _____
6 + 6 = _____   12 − 6 = _____

C.J.'s List

6 + 4 = _____   4 + 6 = _____   10 − 6 = _____
6 + 5 = _____   5 + 6 = _____   11 − 6 = _____
6 + 6 = _____   12 − 6 = _____

Great!

There are twenty important pairs of numbers. Please memorize the sums of these pairs. You will find it very helpful to know them by heart.

1, 2, 3, 4 . . . 20! Wow, it *is* 20 pairs!

Actually, I *have* memorized the sum of these pairs.

9, 2	9, 3	9, 4	9, 5	9, 6	9, 7	9, 8	9, 9
	8, 3	8, 4	8, 5	8, 6	8, 7	8, 8	
		7, 4	7, 5	7, 6	7, 7		
			6, 5	6, 6			

But do you know them well?

Guided Practice

What patterns do you see?

9, 2	9, 3	9, 4	9, 5	9, 6	9, 7	9, 8	9, 9
	8, 3	8, 4	8, 5	8, 6	8, 7	8, 8	
		7, 4	7, 5	7, 6	7, 7		
			6, 5	6, 6			

Quiz 2

Score

Calculate without using your fingers and fill in the answers.

1. $9 + 6 = $ _____   2. $4 + 9 = $ _____   3. $8 + 8 = $ _____   4. $7 + 4 = $ _____   5. $5 + 6 = $ _____

6. $2 + 9 = $ _____   7. $4 + 8 = $ _____   8. $7 + 5 = $ _____   9. $3 + 8 = $ _____   10. $7 + 5 = $ _____

11. $13 - 7 = $ _____   12. $12 - 6 = $ _____   13. $15 - 6 = $ _____   14. $17 - 9 = $ _____   15. $11 - 2 = $ _____

16. $11 - 3 = $ _____   17. $14 - 6 = $ _____   18. $16 - 8 = $ _____   19. $18 - 9 = $ _____   20. $12 - 4 = $ _____

21. $5 + $ _____ $= 12$ 22. $6 + $ _____ $= 12$ 23. $7 + $ _____ $= 12$ 24. $4 + $ _____ $= 12$ 25. $8 + $ _____ $= 12$

26. $15 - $ _____ $= 6$ 27. $15 - $ _____ $= 5$ 28. $15 - $ _____ $= 8$ 29. $15 - $ _____ $= 7$ 30. $15 - $ _____ $= 9$

Calculate the answers. Then write three other versions of each equation.

31.	32.	33.	34.	35.
$8 + 7 = $ _____	$7 + 6 = $ _____	$9 + 8 = $ _____	$13 - 6 = $ _____	$12 - 4 = $ _____
_____	_____	_____	_____	_____
_____	_____	_____	_____	_____
_____	_____	_____	_____	_____

Draw a model and write a mathematical expression to represent this word problem. Then calculate and answer the question.

36. Tom and his brother wrote 15 poems during their summer vacation. Tom wrote 8 of them. How many poems did Tom's brother write?

_____

Model:

Mathematical expression:

Challenge Yourself

37. $60 + 60 = $ _____

38. $70 + 70 = $ _____

39. $80 + 40 = $ _____

40. $90 + 50 = $ _____

41. $50 + 40 = $ _____

42. $15 + 80 + 20 = $ _____

43. $29 + 90 + 10 = $ _____

44. $70 + 40 + 1 = $ _____

45. $20 + 50 + 50 = $ _____

1-11 Which is easier?

Mathematical Conversation

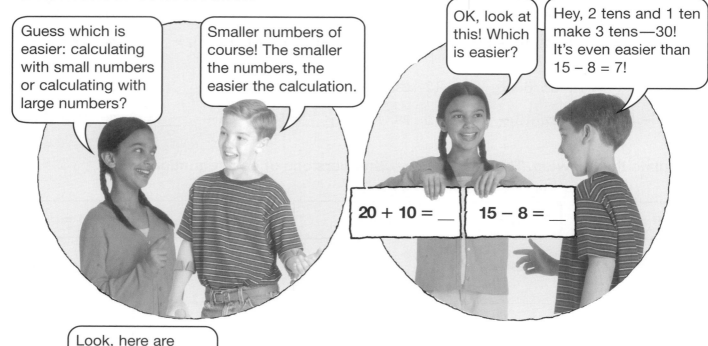

Guess which is easier: calculating with small numbers or calculating with large numbers?

Smaller numbers of course! The smaller the numbers, the easier the calculation.

OK, look at this! Which is easier?

Hey, 2 tens and 1 ten make 3 tens—30! It's even easier than 15 − 8 = 7!

20 + 10 = __   15 − 8 = __

Look, here are some calculations with large numbers.

40 + 40 = ____   70 + 10 = ____   50 − 30 = ____

When you use the real names . . .

. . . these are simple!

Simple questions don't always have simple answers.

Guided Practice

Calculate and fill in the answers. Use the real names for the numbers to help you.

A. 30 + 20 = ____   B. 80 − 20 = ____   C. 35 + 21 = ____   D. 99 − 31 = ____

Lesson 1–11 Exercises

Calculate without using your fingers and fill in the answers.

1. $2 + 2 = $ _____
2. $5 + 3 = $ _____
3. $1 + 5 = $ _____
4. $4 + 3 = $ _____

5. $20 + 20 = $ _____
6. $50 + 30 = $ _____
7. $10 + 50 = $ _____
8. $40 + 30 = $ _____

9. $30 + 31 = $ _____
10. $40 + 14 = $ _____
11. $50 + 42 = $ _____
12. $10 + 83 = $ _____

13. $22 + 52 = $ _____
14. $73 + 23 = $ _____
15. $34 + 34 = $ _____
16. $65 + 11 = $ _____

17. $8 - 3 = $ _____
18. $4 - 1 = $ _____
19. $5 - 2 = $ _____
20. $9 - 3 = $ _____

21. $80 - 30 = $ _____
22. $40 - 10 = $ _____
23. $50 - 20 = $ _____
24. $90 - 30 = $ _____

25. $78 - 50 = $ _____
26. $67 - 30 = $ _____
27. $89 - 60 = $ _____
28. $95 - 20 = $ _____

29. $38 - 24 = $ _____
30. $43 - 21 = $ _____
31. $57 - 56 = $ _____
32. $70 - 70 = $ _____

33. $30 + 50 = $ _____
34. $20 + 70 = $ _____
35. $30 + 40 = $ _____
36. $60 + 30 = $ _____

37. $80 - 20 = $ _____
38. $50 - 10 = $ _____
39. $90 - 80 = $ _____
40. $70 - 40 = $ _____

41. $2 + 2 + 2 = $ _____
42. $20 + 20 + 20 = $ _____

43. $3 + 3 + 3 = $ _____
44. $30 + 30 + 30 = $ _____

45. $10 + 10 - 5 = $ _____
46. $20 + 2 - 1 = $ _____

47. $10 - 7 - 3 = $ _____
48. $40 - 2 - 8 = $ _____

Word Problems

Draw a model and write a mathematical expression to represent each problem.
Then calculate and answer the questions.

49. A white hen laid 20 eggs. A black hen laid 30 eggs. How many eggs did the two hens lay in all? _____

    Model:

    Mathematical expression:

50. Ping's brother weighed 10 pounds two years ago. Now he weighs 30 pounds. How many pounds did he gain? _____

    Model:
    Mathematical expression:

Reflection and Discussion

Do you think computing $20 + 20$ is easier than computing $8 + 6$? Why?

23

1-12   Let's work on some hard computations!

Mathematical Conversation

These computations are a bit harder than the ones we did in the last lesson.

You know what? What we learned before, the trick for computing with 9, would help!

Yes! Good for you!

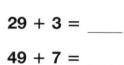

29 + 3 = _____

49 + 7 = _____

32 − 9 = _____

57 − 9 = _____

Here are more computations.

I have two ways to do 48 + 8.

I have two ways to do 95 − 7.

48 + 8 = _____

69 + 6 = _____

37 + 5 = _____

52 − 3 = _____

95 − 7 = _____

Way 1:
8 + 8 = 16 and
40 + 16 = 56

Way 2:
48 + 2 = 50 and
50 + 6 = 56

Way 1:
15 − 7 = 8 and
80 + 8 = 88

Way 2:
95 − 5 = 90 and
90 − 2 = 88

What is your strategy for doing these computations?

Guided Practice

Do these calculations and fill in the answers.

A. 38 + 4 = _____   B. 92 − 3 = _____   C. 75 + 6 = _____   D. 64 − 5 = _____

Lesson 1–12 Exercises

Calculate without using your fingers and fill in the answers.

1. $39 + 2 =$ _____
2. $58 + 3 =$ _____
3. $65 + 5 =$ _____
4. $27 + 4 =$ _____
5. $26 + 5 =$ _____
6. $47 + 4 =$ _____
7. $18 + 5 =$ _____
8. $38 + 3 =$ _____

9. $31 + 9 =$ _____
10. $32 + 9 =$ _____
11. $33 + 9 =$ _____
12. $34 + 9 =$ _____
13. $23 + 8 =$ _____
14. $55 + 6 =$ _____
15. $72 + 9 =$ _____
16. $66 + 4 =$ _____

17. $21 - 3 =$ _____
18. $24 - 5 =$ _____
19. $33 - 6 =$ _____
20. $92 - 3 =$ _____
21. $84 - 6 =$ _____
22. $77 - 9 =$ _____
23. $51 - 4 =$ _____
24. $34 - 8 =$ _____

25. $43 - 5 =$ _____
26. $56 - 7 =$ _____
27. $36 - 8 =$ _____
28. $85 - 6 =$ _____
29. $32 - 7 =$ _____
30. $43 - 6 =$ _____
31. $54 - 9 =$ _____
32. $90 - 8 =$ _____

33. $60 + 30 =$ _____
34. $40 + 20 =$ _____
35. $40 + 40 =$ _____
36. $70 + 30 =$ _____
37. $80 - 60 =$ _____
38. $50 - 40 =$ _____
39. $90 - 30 =$ _____
40. $60 - 50 =$ _____

41. $2 + 7 + 8 =$ _____
42. $29 + 3 + 3 =$ _____
43. $3 + 9 + 7 =$ _____
44. $15 + 6 + 9 =$ _____
45. $22 + 10 - 2 =$ _____
46. $20 + 7 - 6 =$ _____
47. $18 - 8 - 3 =$ _____
48. $32 - 3 - 9 =$ _____

Word Problems

Draw a model and write a mathematical expression to represent each problem.
Then calculate and answer the questions.

49. C.J. hid 35 marbles. His sister found 7. How many marbles are still hidden? _____

    Model:

    Mathematical expression:

50. Ana's mom picked 22 tomatoes and 6 cucumbers. How many more tomatoes are there than cucumbers?

    _____

    Model:

    Mathematical expression:

Reflection and Discussion

What is your strategy for calculating $48 + 6$?

1-13   One step further!

Mathematical Conversation

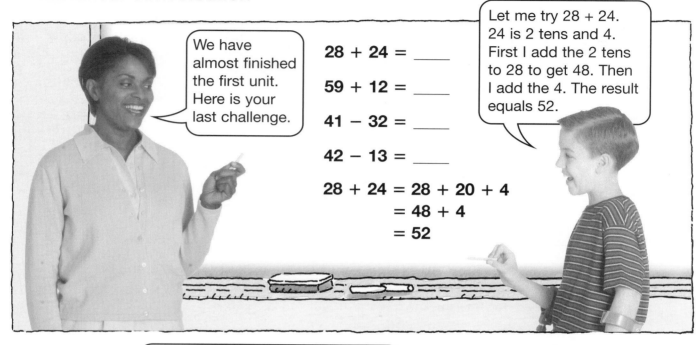

We have almost finished the first unit. Here is your last challenge.

Let me try 28 + 24. 24 is 2 tens and 4. First I add the 2 tens to 28 to get 48. Then I add the 4. The result equals 52.

28 + 24 = ____

59 + 12 = ____

41 − 32 = ____

42 − 13 = ____

$$28 + 24 = 28 + 20 + 4$$
$$= 48 + 4$$
$$= 52$$

I'll try 41 − 32. 32 is 3 tens and 2. I first subtract 30 from 41 and get 11. Then I subtract the 2 and get 9.

$$41 - 32 = 41 - 30 - 2$$
$$= 11 - 2$$
$$= 9$$

Do you want to try, too?

Oh, yes!

Guided Practice

Try these calculations and fill in the answers.

A. 38 + 24 = ____   **B.** 92 − 13 = ____   **C.** 75 + 16 = ____   **D.** 64 − 25 = ____

Lesson 1–13 Exercises

Calculate without using your fingers and fill in the answers.

1. 29 + 12 = ____
2. 18 + 13 = ____
3. 15 + 16 = ____
4. 26 + 14 = ____

5. 38 + 13 = ____
6. 17 + 24 = ____
7. 18 + 15 = ____
8. 38 + 13 = ____

9. 11 + 19 = ____
10. 12 + 19 = ____
11. 13 + 19 = ____
12. 14 + 19 = ____

13. 23 + 18 = ____
14. 55 + 26 = ____
15. 42 + 29 = ____
16. 36 + 24 = ____

17. 21 − 11 = ____
18. 25 − 15 = ____
19. 33 − 13 = ____
20. 46 − 16 = ____

21. 74 − 24 = ____
22. 47 − 27 = ____
23. 48 − 38 = ____
24. 84 − 14 = ____

25. 43 − 15 = ____
26. 56 − 17 = ____
27. 36 − 28 = ____
28. 85 − 26 = ____

29. 32 − 27 = ____
30. 43 − 26 = ____
31. 54 − 29 = ____
32. 90 − 38 = ____

33. 60 + 24 = ____
34. 40 + 45 = ____
35. 50 + 29 = ____
36. 50 + 36 = ____

37. 80 − 11 = ____
38. 50 − 22 = ____
39. 90 − 9 = ____
40. 60 − 5 = ____

41. 12 + 4 + 3 = ____
42. 29 + 1 + 4 = ____

43. 11 + 9 + 5 = ____
44. 16 + 4 + 2 = ____

45. 22 + 12 − 2 = ____
46. 20 + 6 − 6 = ____

47. 12 − 2 − 3 = ____
48. 34 − 9 − 9 = ____

Word Problems

**Draw a model and write a mathematical expression to represent each problem.
Then calculate and answer the questions.**

49. Juan had 59 books. Mary gave him 12 books. Now how many does Juan have? _____

Model:

Mathematical expression:

50. Ping has 31 silkworms. She sees that 19 of them have spun cocoons. How many have not yet spun cocoons? _____

Model:

Mathematical expression:

Reflection and Discussion

What is your strategy for calculating 64 − 25?

1-14   Unit 1 Review

Mathematical Conversation

Unit 1 Review Exercises

Build your own across-10 facts neighborhood. Don't copy C.J.'s.

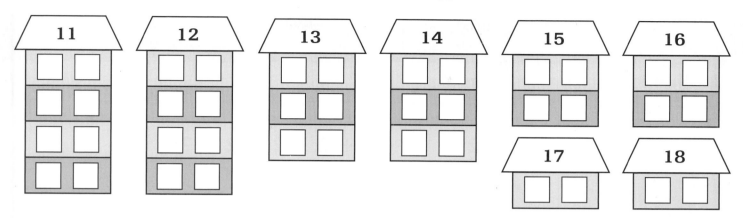

Build a within-10 facts neighborhood.

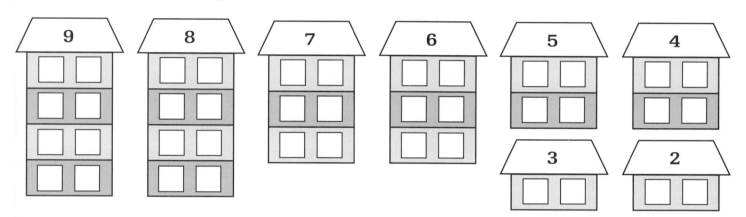

Calculate without using your fingers and fill in the answers.

1. _____ + 6 = 10   2. _____ + 5 = 10   3. _____ + 8 = 10

4. 10 − _____ = 9   5. 10 − _____ = 7   6. 10 − _____ = 6

7. _____ + 4 = 10   8. _____ + 6 = 10

9. 10 − _____ = 8   10. 10 − _____ = 5

11. 5 + 4 = _____   12. 7 + 8 = _____   13. 8 − 3 = _____   14. 12 − 6 = _____   15. 13 − 4 = _____

16. 20 + 20 = _____   17. 40 + 30 = _____   18. 28 + 10 = _____   19. 70 + 14 = _____   20. 56 + 30 = _____

21. 34 + 21 = _____   22. 51 + 32 = _____   23. 72 + 15 = _____   24. 38 + 21 = _____   25. 45 + 13 = _____

26. 5 + 24 + 5 = _____   27. 19 + 3 + 7 = _____   28. 3 + 18 + 7 = _____   29. 45 + 3 + 2 = _____

30. 24 + 10 − 4 = _____   31. 20 + 7 − 6 = _____   32. 38 − 8 − 30 = _____   33. 32 − 2 − 9 = _____

2-1   What does 6 × 2 mean?

Mathematical Conversation

Guided Practice

Write two multiplication equations for each group of dots.

A. • • •   B. • • • •   C. • • • • •   D. • • • • • • •   E. • • • • • • • •   F. • • • • • • • • •
   • • •   • • • •   • • • • •   • • • • • • •   • • • • • • • •   • • • • • • • • •

_____   _____   _____   _____   _____   _____

_____   _____   _____   _____   _____   _____

Lesson 2-1 Exercises

Compare the two tables, line by line. How do we get the "2 Times" table from the "Times 2" table? Memorize the two tables.

"TIMES 2" TABLE	"2 TIMES" TABLE
Two twos make 4.	Two twos make 4.
Three twos make 6.	Two threes make 6.
Four twos make 8.	Two fours make 8.
Five twos make 10.	Two fives make 10.
Six twos make 12.	Two sixes make 12.
Seven twos make 14.	Two sevens make 14.
Eight twos make 16.	Two eights make 16.
Nine twos make 18.	Two nines make 18.

Investigate this multiplication table. Fill in the facts you learned today. Then lightly color the boxes.

2 × 2 =	2 × 3 =	2 × 4 =	2 × 5 =	2 × 6 =	2 × 7 =	2 × 8 =	2 × 9 =
3 × 2 =	3 × 3 =	3 × 4 =	3 × 5 =	3 × 6 =	3 × 7 =	3 × 8 =	3 × 9 =
4 × 2 =	4 × 3 =	4 × 4 =	4 × 5 =	4 × 6 =	4 × 7 =	4 × 8 =	4 × 9 =
5 × 2 =	5 × 3 =	5 × 4 =	5 × 5 =	5 × 6 =	5 × 7 =	5 × 8 =	5 × 9 =
6 × 2 =	6 × 3 =	6 × 4 =	6 × 5 =	6 × 6 =	6 × 7 =	6 × 8 =	6 × 9 =
7 × 2 =	7 × 3 =	7 × 4 =	7 × 5 =	7 × 6 =	7 × 7 =	7 × 8 =	7 × 9 =
8 × 2 =	8 × 3 =	8 × 4 =	8 × 5 =	8 × 6 =	8 × 7 =	8 × 8 =	8 × 9 =
9 × 2 =	9 × 3 =	9 × 4 =	9 × 5 =	9 × 6 =	9 × 7 =	9 × 8 =	9 × 9 =

Word Problems

Write a mathematical expression to solve each problem. Use the models to help you.

1. Ms. Park used 2 baskets to carry apples. She put 8 apples in each basket. How many apples did she have? _____

Mathematical expression:

2. A bird has 2 wings. How many wings do 6 birds have? _____ __

Mathematical expression:

Reflection and Discussion

What is the difference in meaning between 3 × 1 and 1 × 3? What does each one equal?

31

Warm-up Exercises

6 + 4 = ____   7 + 6 = ____   6 + 5 = ____   8 + 8 = ____

7 − 2 = ____   12 − 3 = ____   9 − 4 = ____   10 − 7 = ____

2-2   Why does 3 × 5 = 5 × 3?

Mathematical Conversation

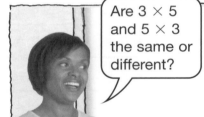

These two expressions look so different! I never thought they were related!

5 + 5 + 5 = ?   3 + 3 + 3 + 3 + 3 = ?

Here is the dot-chart that relates your two expressions.

Are 3 × 5 and 5 × 3 the same or different?

They are different, because 3 × 5 means 3 fives, but 5 × 3 means 5 threes.

They are the same, because they have the same products.

With whom do you agree, Lily or Danny?

Guided Practice

Write two multiplication equations for each group of dots.

A.   B.    C.    D.    E.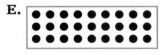

Lesson 2–2 Exercises

Compare the two tables, line by line. How do we get the "3 Times" table from the "Times 3" table? Memorize both tables.

"TIMES 3" TABLE	"3 TIMES" TABLE
Two threes make 6.	Three twos make 6.
Three threes make 9.	Three threes make 9.
Four threes make 12.	Three fours make 12.
Five threes make 15.	Three fives make 15.
Six threes make 18.	Three sixes make 18.
Seven threes make 21.	Three sevens make 21.
Eight threes make 24.	Three eights make 24.
Nine threes make 27.	Three nines make 27.

Fill in and shade the multiplication facts for 2 and 3. Use a different color for the facts you learned today.

2 × 2 =	2 × 3 =	2 × 4 =	2 × 5 =	2 × 6 =	2 × 7 =	2 × 8 =	2 × 9 =
3 × 2 =	3 × 3 =	3 × 4 =	3 × 5 =	3 × 6 =	3 × 7 =	3 × 8 =	3 × 9 =
4 × 2 =	4 × 3 =	4 × 4 =	4 × 5 =	4 × 6 =	4 × 7 =	4 × 8 =	4 × 9 =
5 × 2 =	5 × 3 =	5 × 4 =	5 × 5 =	5 × 6 =	5 × 7 =	5 × 8 =	5 × 9 =
6 × 2 =	6 × 3 =	6 × 4 =	6 × 5 =	6 × 6 =	6 × 7 =	6 × 8 =	6 × 9 =
7 × 2 =	7 × 3 =	7 × 4 =	7 × 5 =	7 × 6 =	7 × 7 =	7 × 8 =	7 × 9 =
8 × 2 =	8 × 3 =	8 × 4 =	8 × 5 =	8 × 6 =	8 × 7 =	8 × 8 =	8 × 9 =
9 × 2 =	9 × 3 =	9 × 4 =	9 × 5 =	9 × 6 =	9 × 7 =	9 × 8 =	9 × 9 =

Word Problems

Write a mathematical expression to solve each problem. Use the models to help you.

1. There are 3 wheels on a tricycle. How many wheels are there on 4 tricycles? _____

Mathematical expression:

2. For a Thanksgiving food drive, each student brought 7 cans of food. How many cans did 3 students bring?

_____

Mathematical expression:

Reflection and Discussion

If you calculate 3 × 4 and 4 × 3, will you get the same product? Why?

2-3 Can you make the times table for 4?

Mathematical Conversation

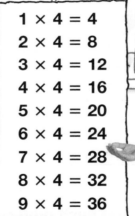

Guided Practice

Write two multiplication equations for each group of dots.

A. 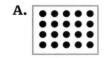   B. 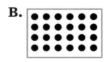   C. 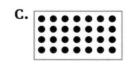   D. 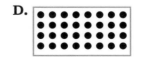   E.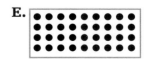

_____   _____   _____   _____   _____

_____   _____   _____   _____   _____

Lesson 2–3 Exercises

Compare the two tables, line by line. How do we get the "4 Times" table from the "Times 4" table? Memorize both tables.

"TIMES 4" TABLE	"4 TIMES" TABLE
Two fours make 8.	Four twos make 8.
Three fours make 12.	Four threes make 12.
Four fours make 16.	Four fours make 16.
Five fours make 20.	Four fives make 20.
Six fours make 24.	Four sixes make 24.
Seven fours make 28.	Four sevens make 28.
Eight fours make 32.	Four eights make 32.
Nine fours make 36.	Four nines make 36.

Fill in and shade the facts you have learned so far. Use a different color for the facts you learned today.

2 × 2 =	2 × 3 =	2 × 4 =	2 × 5 =	2 × 6 =	2 × 7 =	2 × 8 =	2 × 9 =
3 × 2 =	3 × 3 =	3 × 4 =	3 × 5 =	3 × 6 =	3 × 7 =	3 × 8 =	3 × 9 =
4 × 2 =	4 × 3 =	4 × 4 =	4 × 5 =	4 × 6 =	4 × 7 =	4 × 8 =	4 × 9 =
5 × 2 =	5 × 3 =	5 × 4 =	5 × 5 =	5 × 6 =	5 × 7 =	5 × 8 =	5 × 9 =
6 × 2 =	6 × 3 =	6 × 4 =	6 × 5 =	6 × 6 =	6 × 7 =	6 × 8 =	6 × 9 =
7 × 2 =	7 × 3 =	7 × 4 =	7 × 5 =	7 × 6 =	7 × 7 =	7 × 8 =	7 × 9 =
8 × 2 =	8 × 3 =	8 × 4 =	8 × 5 =	8 × 6 =	8 × 7 =	8 × 8 =	8 × 9 =
9 × 2 =	9 × 3 =	9 × 4 =	9 × 5 =	9 × 6 =	9 × 7 =	9 × 8 =	9 × 9 =

Word Problems

Write a mathematical expression to solve each problem. Use the models to help you.

1. A chair has 4 legs. How many legs do 4 chairs have? _____

Mathematical expression:

2. One movie ticket costs $7. Lily buys 4 tickets. How much does she pay?

Mathematical expression:

Reflection and Discussion

The models for the two word problems on this page look similar. Why then do the problems have different answers?

2-4   Can you find a pattern?

Mathematical Conversation

Today we are going to learn the times tables for 5.

We knew you would say that! We worked together again to make the tables.

Here is my "Times 5" table.

Look, here is my "5 Times" table.

Do you notice a pattern in the two tables? Can you explain it?

I see the pattern, but I want you to find it and explain it yourself.

Do I get any hints?

1 × 5 = 5	5 × 1 = 5
2 × 5 = 10	5 × 2 = 10
3 × 5 = 15	5 × 3 = 15
4 × 5 = 20	5 × 4 = 20
5 × 5 = 25	5 × 5 = 25
6 × 5 = 30	5 × 6 = 30
7 × 5 = 35	5 × 7 = 35
8 × 5 = 40	5 × 8 = 40
9 × 5 = 45	5 × 9 = 45

Guided Practice

Write two multiplications equations for each group of dots.

A.   B.   C. 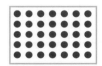   D. 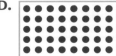   E.

_____   _____   _____   _____   _____

_____   _____   _____   _____   _____

Lesson 2–4 Exercises

Compare the two tables, line by line. How do we get the "5 Times" table from the "Times 5" table? Memorize both tables.

"TIMES 5" TABLE	"5 TIMES" TABLE
Two fives make 10.	Five twos make 10.
Three fives make 15.	Five threes make 15.
Four fives make 20.	Five fours make 20.
Five fives make 25.	Five fives make 25.
Six fives make 30.	Five sixes make 30.
Seven fives make 35.	Five sevens make 35.
Eight fives make 40.	Five eights make 40.
Nines fives make 45.	Five nines make 45.

Fill in and shade the facts you have learned so far. Use a different color for the facts you learned today.

$2 \times 2 =$	$2 \times 3 =$	$2 \times 4 =$	$2 \times 5 =$	$2 \times 6 =$	$2 \times 7 =$	$2 \times 8 =$	$2 \times 9 =$
$3 \times 2 =$	$3 \times 3 =$	$3 \times 4 =$	$3 \times 5 =$	$3 \times 6 =$	$3 \times 7 =$	$3 \times 8 =$	$3 \times 9 =$
$4 \times 2 =$	$4 \times 3 =$	$4 \times 4 =$	$4 \times 5 =$	$4 \times 6 =$	$4 \times 7 =$	$4 \times 8 =$	$4 \times 9 =$
$5 \times 2 =$	$5 \times 3 =$	$5 \times 4 =$	$5 \times 5 =$	$5 \times 6 =$	$5 \times 7 =$	$5 \times 8 =$	$5 \times 9 =$
$6 \times 2 =$	$6 \times 3 =$	$6 \times 4 =$	$6 \times 5 =$	$6 \times 6 =$	$6 \times 7 =$	$6 \times 8 =$	$6 \times 9 =$
$7 \times 2 =$	$7 \times 3 =$	$7 \times 4 =$	$7 \times 5 =$	$7 \times 6 =$	$7 \times 7 =$	$7 \times 8 =$	$7 \times 9 =$
$8 \times 2 =$	$8 \times 3 =$	$8 \times 4 =$	$8 \times 5 =$	$8 \times 6 =$	$8 \times 7 =$	$8 \times 8 =$	$8 \times 9 =$
$9 \times 2 =$	$9 \times 3 =$	$9 \times 4 =$	$9 \times 5 =$	$9 \times 6 =$	$9 \times 7 =$	$9 \times 8 =$	$9 \times 9 =$

Word Problems

Write a mathematical expression to solve each problem. Use the models to help you.

1. One kind of star has 5 points. How many points do 6 of these stars have? _____

Mathematical expression:

2. Danny's mom needs 8 cups of flour to bake a cake. If she makes 5 cakes, how many cups of flour will she use? _____

Mathematical expression:

Reflection and Discussion

Without calculating 12×5, figure out what the digit in the ones place will be. How do you know?

2-5   Review, Reflection, and Quiz 3

Mathematical Conversation

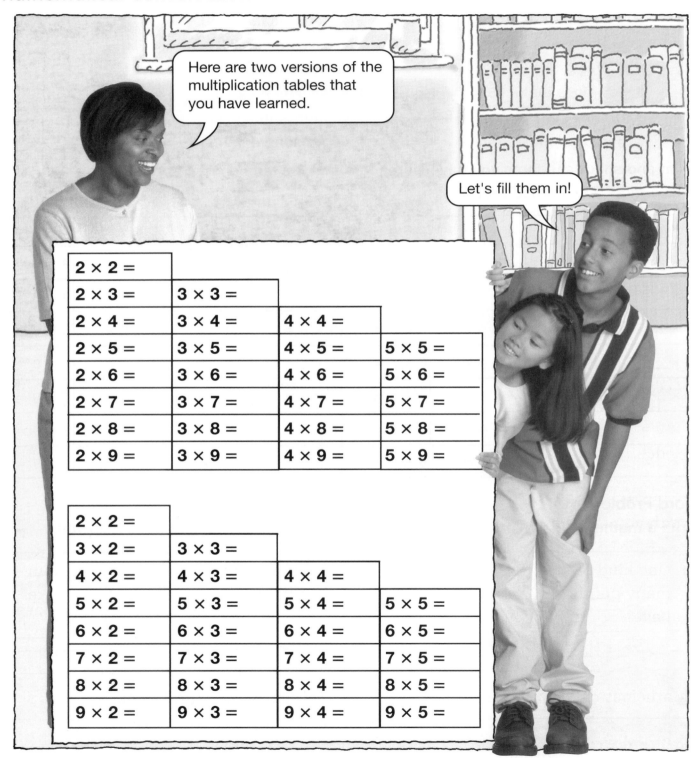

Quiz 3

Calculate and fill in the answers.

1. $2 \times 2 =$ _____
2. $2 \times 3 =$ _____
3. $2 \times 5 =$ _____
4. $2 \times 7 =$ _____
5. $2 \times 8 =$ _____

6. $3 \times 2 =$ _____
7. $6 \times 2 =$ _____
8. $4 \times 2 =$ _____
9. $9 \times 2 =$ _____
10. $5 \times 2 =$ _____

11. $3 \times 3 =$ _____
12. $3 \times 5 =$ _____
13. $3 \times 4 =$ _____
14. $3 \times 8 =$ _____
15. $3 \times 6 =$ _____

16. $7 \times 3 =$ _____
17. $9 \times 3 =$ _____
18. $4 \times 3 =$ _____
19. $5 \times 3 =$ _____
20. $8 \times 3 =$ _____

21. $4 \times 2 =$ _____
22. $4 \times 4 =$ _____
23. $4 \times 6 =$ _____
24. $4 \times 8 =$ _____
25. $4 \times 9 =$ _____

26. $5 \times 4 =$ _____
27. $2 \times 4 =$ _____
28. $6 \times 4 =$ _____
29. $7 \times 4 =$ _____
30. $9 \times 4 =$ _____

31. $5 \times 6 =$ _____
32. $5 \times 7 =$ _____
33. $5 \times 1 =$ _____
34. $5 \times 9 =$ _____
35. $5 \times 8 =$ _____

36. $7 \times 5 =$ _____
37. $4 \times 5 =$ _____
38. $5 \times 5 =$ _____
39. $6 \times 5 =$ _____
40. $7 \times 5 =$ _____

Word Problem

Draw a model and write a mathematical expression to represent the problem.
Then calculate and answer the question.

41. Ana's class has 4 math groups. Each math group has 5 students.
    How many students are there? _____

Model:

Mathematical expression:

Challenge Yourself

42. $2 \times 20 =$ _____
43. $3 \times 30 =$ _____
44. $4 \times 2 \times 2 =$ _____
45. $3 \times 3 \times 3 =$ _____

2-6   What is the inverse of multiplication?

Mathematical Conversation

I think that today we are going to learn the times tables for 6. I worked out a short version— with only four lines!

$6 \times 6 = 36$
$6 \times 7 = 42$
$6 \times 8 = 48$
$6 \times 9 = 54$

That's great! I have a question, Lily. We learned that subtraction is the inverse of addition. Does multiplication have an inverse, too?

What's the inverse of multiplication? Interesting question! Let's use addition and subtraction to get some ideas . . .

If we have an addition equation with a missing addend before the equals sign, we can use subtraction to find the number.

I've got an idea. The inverse of multiplication may be the way to find a missing factor before the equals sign in a multiplication equation!

$3 +$ _____ $= 5$ _____ $+ 1 = 6$
$5 - 3 = 2$ $6 - 1 = 5$

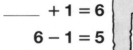

$2 \times$ _____ $= 10$ _____ $\times 4 = 24$

Good for you! The operation we use to find a missing factor in a multiplication is called division. For example, to find the missing factor in $6 \times$ _____ $= 42$, we do the division, $42 \div 6 = 7$.

We can use the multiplication tables to do division! Can you fill in this blank? _____ $\times 7 = 42$

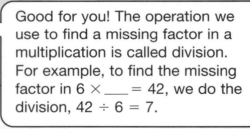

Guided Practice

Complete each multiplication fact. Draw dot charts to represent the equations and then write related division equations.

A. $6 \times 6 =$ **36**      **B.** $6 \times 7 =$ **C.** $6 \times 8 =$ **D.** $6 \times 9 =$

$36 \div 6 = 6$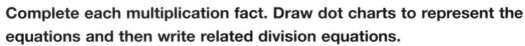

Lesson 2–6 Exercises

Compare the two tables, line by line. How do we get the "6 Times" table from the "Times 6" table? Memorize both tables.

"TIMES 6" TABLE	"6 TIMES" TABLE
Two sixes make 12.	Six twos make 12.
Three sixes make 18.	Six threes make 18.
Four sixes make 24.	Six fours make 24.
Five sixes make 30.	Six fives make 30.
Six sixes make 36.	Six sixes make 36.
Seven sixes make 42.	Six sevens make 42.
Eight sixes make 48.	Six eights make 48.
Nine sixes make 54.	Six nines make 54.

Fill in and shade the facts you have learned so far. Use a different color for facts you learned today.

2 × 2 =	2 × 3 =	2 × 4 =	2 × 5 =	2 × 6 =	2 × 7 =	2 × 8 =	2 × 9 =
3 × 2 =	3 × 3 =	3 × 4 =	3 × 5 =	3 × 6 =	3 × 7 =	3 × 8 =	3 × 9 =
4 × 2 =	4 × 3 =	4 × 4 =	4 × 5 =	4 × 6 =	4 × 7 =	4 × 8 =	4 × 9 =
5 × 2 =	5 × 3 =	5 × 4 =	5 × 5 =	5 × 6 =	5 × 7 =	5 × 8 =	5 × 9 =
6 × 2 =	6 × 3 =	6 × 4 =	6 × 5 =	6 × 6 =	6 × 7 =	6 × 8 =	6 × 9 =
7 × 2 =	7 × 3 =	7 × 4 =	7 × 5 =	7 × 6 =	7 × 7 =	7 × 8 =	7 × 9 =
8 × 2 =	8 × 3 =	8 × 4 =	8 × 5 =	8 × 6 =	8 × 7 =	8 × 8 =	8 × 9 =
9 × 2 =	9 × 3 =	9 × 4 =	9 × 5 =	9 × 6 =	9 × 7 =	9 × 8 =	9 × 9 =

Word Problems

Write a mathematical expression to solve each problem. Use the models to help you.

1. An ant has 6 legs. How many legs do 9 ants have? _____ _ __

6	6	6	6	6	6	6	6	6

⎣————————— ? —————————⎦

Mathematical expression:

2. Maria has $48. A book costs $6. How many books can she buy? _____

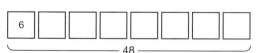

⎣————————— 48 —————————⎦

Mathematical expression:

Reflection and Discussion

Compare the two pairs of inverse operations: addition/subtraction and multiplication/division. What pattern do you see?

2-7   How are multiplication and division related?

Mathematical Conversation

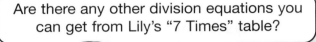

Are there any other division equations you can get from Lily's "7 Times" table?

This short version of the "7 Times" table has only three lines.

So it also means that:

Let's see, there should be two more.

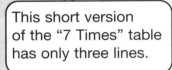

7 × 7 = 49
7 × 8 = 56
7 × 9 = 63

49 ÷ 7 = 7
56 ÷ 7 = 8
63 ÷ 7 = 9

56 ÷ 8 = 7
63 ÷ 9 = 7

Here's what I notice. In multiplication and addition equations, the first two numbers can trade places. In division and subtraction equations, however, the last two numbers can trade places.

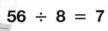

If $a \times b = c$, then $b \times a = c$

If $a + b = c$, then $b + a = c$

If $c \div b = a$, then $c \div a = b$

If $c - b = a$, then $c - a = b$

Do you notice that most multiplication equations have four different versions?

I know! There are two multiplication and two division versions.

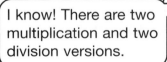

Guided Practice

Complete each multiplication fact. Then write three other versions.

A. 7 × 6 = **42**

＿＿＿＿＿＿＿＿＿

＿＿＿＿＿＿＿＿＿

＿＿＿＿＿＿＿＿＿

B. 7 × 8 =

＿＿＿＿＿＿＿＿＿

＿＿＿＿＿＿＿＿＿

＿＿＿＿＿＿＿＿＿

C. 7 × 9 =

＿＿＿＿＿＿＿＿＿

＿＿＿＿＿＿＿＿＿

＿＿＿＿＿＿＿＿＿

Lesson 2–7 Exercises

Compare the two tables, line by line. How do we get the "7 times" table from the "times 7" table? Memorize both tables.

"TIMES 7" TABLE	"7 TIMES" TABLE
Two sevens make 14.	Seven twos make 14.
Three sevens make 21.	Seven threes make 21.
Four sevens make 28.	Seven fours make 28.
Five sevens make 35.	Seven fives make 35.
Six sevens make 42.	Seven sixes make 42.
Seven sevens make 49.	Seven sevens make 49.
Eight sevens make 56.	Seven eights make 56.
Nine sevens make 63.	Seven nines make 63.

Fill in and shade the facts you have learned so far. Use a different color for facts you learned today.

2 × 2 =	2 × 3 =	2 × 4 =	2 × 5 =	2 × 6 =	2 × 7 =	2 × 8 =	2 × 9 =
3 × 2 =	3 × 3 =	3 × 4 =	3 × 5 =	3 × 6 =	3 × 7 =	3 × 8 =	3 × 9 =
4 × 2 =	4 × 3 =	4 × 4 =	4 × 5 =	4 × 6 =	4 × 7 =	4 × 8 =	4 × 9 =
5 × 2 =	5 × 3 =	5 × 4 =	5 × 5 =	5 × 6 =	5 × 7 =	5 × 8 =	5 × 9 =
6 × 2 =	6 × 3 =	6 × 4 =	6 × 5 =	6 × 6 =	6 × 7 =	6 × 8 =	6 × 9 =
7 × 2 =	7 × 3 =	7 × 4 =	7 × 5 =	7 × 6 =	7 × 7 =	7 × 8 =	7 × 9 =
8 × 2 =	8 × 3 =	8 × 4 =	8 × 5 =	8 × 6 =	8 × 7 =	8 × 8 =	8 × 9 =
9 × 2 =	9 × 3 =	9 × 4 =	9 × 5 =	9 × 6 =	9 × 7 =	9 × 8 =	9 × 9 =

Word Problems

Write a mathematical expression to solve each problem. Use the models to help you.

1. A week has 7 days, so how many days do 5 weeks have? _____

7	7	7	7	7

   ⌞———— ? ————⌟

   Mathematical expression:

2. A week has 7 days, so how many weeks does a February with 28 days have?

   _____

   ⌜———— 28 ————⌝

7			

   Mathematical expression:

Reflection and Discussion

How many division equations can you make from 7 × 7 = ? Why?

2-8   How many lines in the times table for 8?

Mathematical Conversation

Guess how many lines we have to memorize in the times table for 8.

I bet there are two.

That's because we started with the tables for small numbers. By now, we have learned a big part of the times tables for large numbers from the times tables for small numbers!

Hmm . . . what if we started by learning times tables in a different order? Say we started with tables for large numbers and ended with tables for small numbers. Then it would be the larger the number, the longer the table!

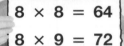

$8 \times 8 = 64$
$8 \times 9 = 72$

Cool! The larger the number, the shorter the table!

It is wise to start with small numbers!

I can see why!

Guided Practice

Complete each multiplication fact. Then write 3 other versions.

A. $8 \times 3 =$ _____   **B.** $8 \times 4 =$ _____   **C.** $8 \times 5 =$ _____   **D.** $8 \times 6 =$ _____   **E.** $8 \times 7 =$ _____

_____   _____   _____   _____   _____

_____   _____   _____   _____   _____

_____   _____   _____   _____   _____

Lesson 2–8 Exercises

Compare the two tables, line by line. How do we get the "8 Times" table from the "Times 8" table? Memorize both tables.

"TIMES 8" TABLE	"8 TIMES" TABLE
Two eights make 16.	Eight twos make 16.
Three eights make 24.	Eight threes make 24.
Four eights make 32.	Eight fours make 32.
Five eights make 40.	Eight fives make 40.
Six eights make 48.	Eight sixes make 48.
Seven eights make 56.	Eight sevens make 56.
Eight eights make 64.	Eight eights make 64.
Nine eights make 72.	Eight nines make 72.

Fill in and shade the facts you have learned so far. Use a different color for facts you learned today.

2 × 2 =	2 × 3 =	2 × 4 =	2 × 5 =	2 × 6 =	2 × 7 =	2 × 8 =	2 × 9 =
3 × 2 =	3 × 3 =	3 × 4 =	3 × 5 =	3 × 6 =	3 × 7 =	3 × 8 =	3 × 9 =
4 × 2 =	4 × 3 =	4 × 4 =	4 × 5 =	4 × 6 =	4 × 7 =	4 × 8 =	4 × 9 =
5 × 2 =	5 × 3 =	5 × 4 =	5 × 5 =	5 × 6 =	5 × 7 =	5 × 8 =	5 × 9 =
6 × 2 =	6 × 3 =	6 × 4 =	6 × 5 =	6 × 6 =	6 × 7 =	6 × 8 =	6 × 9 =
7 × 2 =	7 × 3 =	7 × 4 =	7 × 5 =	7 × 6 =	7 × 7 =	7 × 8 =	7 × 9 =
8 × 2 =	8 × 3 =	8 × 4 =	8 × 5 =	8 × 6 =	8 × 7 =	8 × 8 =	8 × 9 =
9 × 2 =	9 × 3 =	9 × 4 =	9 × 5 =	9 × 6 =	9 × 7 =	9 × 8 =	9 × 9 =

Word Problems

Write a mathematical expression to solve each problem. Use the models to help you.

1. An octopus has 8 tentacles. How many tentacles do 3 octopuses have?

8	8	8

?

Expression:

2. Ms. Park shares 48 sheets of origami paper equally among 8 students. How many sheets does each student receive? _____

48

?

Expression:

Reflection and Discussion

C.J. says "The larger the number, the shorter the table." Do you agree with that statement? Why?

2-9   Finally, the times table for 9!

Mathematical Conversation

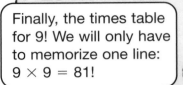

Finally, the times table for 9! We will only have to memorize one line: 9 × 9 = 81!

That's true only if we know the earlier multiplication tables by heart.

Do you remember the patterns for adding and subtracting 9? Why don't you write out the whole times table for 9? See if you can find a pattern there, too.

Here is the whole times table for 9.

9 × 1 = 9	1 × 9 = 9
9 × 2 = 18	2 × 9 = 18
9 × 3 = 27	3 × 9 = 27
9 × 4 = 36	4 × 9 = 36
9 × 5 = 45	5 × 9 = 45
9 × 6 = 54	6 × 9 = 54
9 × 7 = 63	7 × 9 = 63
9 × 8 = 72	8 × 9 = 72
9 × 9 = 81	9 × 9 = 81

I see a pattern! When we multiply a number by 9, we put a zero after the number and subtract the number. For example:

9 × 1 equals 10 − 1, which is   9.
9 × 2 equals 20 − 2, which is 18.
9 × 3 equals 30 − 3, which is 27.

I like Lily's idea! But I think instead of saying "put a zero after the number" she might want to say "multiply the number by 10." Do you agree with me?

Oh, yes!

Guided Practice

Complete each multiplication fact. Then write three other versions.

A. 9 × 4 = _____   **B.** 9 × 5 = _____   **C.** 9 × 6 = _____   **D.** 9 × 7 = _____   **E.** 9 × 8 = _____

_____   _____   _____   _____   _____

_____   _____   _____   _____   _____

_____   _____   _____   _____   _____

Lesson 2–9 Exercises

Compare the two tables, line by line. How do we get the "9 Times" table from the "Times 9" table? Memorize both tables.

"TIMES 9" TABLE

Two nines make 18.

Three nines make 27.

Four nines 36.

Five nines 45.

Six nines make 54.

Seven nines make 63.

Eight nines make 72.

Nine nines make 81.

"9 TIMES" TABLE

Nine twos make 18.

Nine threes make 27.

Nine fours make 36.

Nine fives make 45.

Nine sixes make 54.

Nine sevens make 63.

Nine eights make 72.

Nine nines make 81.

Complete the facts below. Then lightly color the boxes of the facts you learned today.

2 × 2 =	2 × 3 =	2 × 4 =	2 × 5 =	2 × 6 =	2 × 7 =	2 × 8 =	2 × 9 =
3 × 2 =	3 × 3 =	3 × 4 =	3 × 5 =	3 × 6 =	3 × 7 =	3 × 8 =	3 × 9 =
4 × 2 =	4 × 3 =	4 × 4 =	4 × 5 =	4 × 6 =	4 × 7 =	4 × 8 =	4 × 9 =
5 × 2 =	5 × 3 =	5 × 4 =	5 × 5 =	5 × 6 =	5 × 7 =	5 × 8 =	5 × 9 =
6 × 2 =	6 × 3 =	6 × 4 =	6 × 5 =	6 × 6 =	6 × 7 =	6 × 8 =	6 × 9 =
7 × 2 =	7 × 3 =	7 × 4 =	7 × 5 =	7 × 6 =	7 × 7 =	7 × 8 =	7 × 9 =
8 × 2 =	8 × 3 =	8 × 4 =	8 × 5 =	8 × 6 =	8 × 7 =	8 × 8 =	8 × 9 =
9 × 2 =	9 × 3 =	9 × 4 =	9 × 5 =	9 × 6 =	9 × 7 =	9 × 8 =	9 × 9 =

Word Problems

Write a mathematical expression to solve each problem. Use the models to help you.

1. There are 9 books in a complete set of "Little House" books. How many books are there in 6 complete sets of "Little House" books? _____

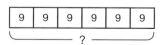

Mathematical expression:

2. Danny arranged 18 chairs in 2 rows. He put the same number of chairs in each row. How many chairs were there in each row? _____

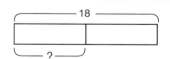

Mathematical expression:

Reflection and Discussion

Can you explain the pattern that Ana found for multiplying by 9?

47

2-10   Review, Reflection, and Quiz 4

Mathematical Conversation

Today we are going to review multiplication tables by doing division.

Cool! Let's try!

2 ÷ 2 =	3 ÷ 3 =	4 ÷ 4 =	5 ÷ 5 =
4 ÷ 2 =	6 ÷ 3 =	8 ÷ 4 =	10 ÷ 5 =
6 ÷ 2 =	9 ÷ 3 =	12 ÷ 4 =	15 ÷ 5 =
8 ÷ 2 =	12 ÷ 3 =	16 ÷ 4 =	20 ÷ 5 =
10 ÷ 2 =	15 ÷ 3 =	20 ÷ 4 =	25 ÷ 5 =
12 ÷ 2 =	18 ÷ 3 =	24 ÷ 4 =	30 ÷ 5 =
14 ÷ 2 =	21 ÷ 3 =	28 ÷ 4 =	35 ÷ 5 =
16 ÷ 2 =	24 ÷ 3 =	32 ÷ 4 =	40 ÷ 5 =

6 ÷ 6 =	7 ÷ 7 =	8 ÷ 8 =	9 ÷ 9 =
12 ÷ 6 =	14 ÷ 7 =	16 ÷ 8 =	18 ÷ 9 =
18 ÷ 6 =	21 ÷ 7 =	24 ÷ 8 =	27 ÷ 9 =
24 ÷ 6 =	28 ÷ 7 =	32 ÷ 8 =	36 ÷ 9 =
30 ÷ 6 =	35 ÷ 7 =	40 ÷ 8 =	45 ÷ 9 =
36 ÷ 6 =	42 ÷ 7 =	48 ÷ 8 =	54 ÷ 9 =
42 ÷ 6 =	49 ÷ 7 =	56 ÷ 8 =	63 ÷ 9 =
48 ÷ 6 =	56 ÷ 7 =	64 ÷ 8 =	72 ÷ 9 =

Quiz 4

Calculate and fill in the answers.

1. $6 \times 6 =$ _____ 2. $6 \times 3 =$ _____ 3. $6 \times 5 =$ _____ 4. $6 \times 7 =$ _____ 5. $6 \times 8 =$ _____

6. $3 \times 6 =$ _____ 7. $2 \times 6 =$ _____ 8. $4 \times 6 =$ _____ 9. $9 \times 6 =$ _____ 10. $5 \times 6 =$ _____

11. $7 \times 7 =$ _____ 12. $7 \times 5 =$ _____ 13. $7 \times 4 =$ _____ 14. $7 \times 8 =$ _____ 15. $7 \times 6 =$ _____

16. $3 \times 7 =$ _____ 17. $2 \times 7 =$ _____ 18. $4 \times 7 =$ _____ 19. $5 \times 7 =$ _____ 20. $8 \times 7 =$ _____

21. $8 \times 8 =$ _____ 22. $8 \times 4 =$ _____ 23. $8 \times 6 =$ _____ 24. $8 \times 8 =$ _____ 25. $8 \times 9 =$ _____

26. $5 \times 8 =$ _____ 27. $2 \times 8 =$ _____ 28. $5 \times 8 =$ _____ 29. $4 \times 9 =$ _____ 30. $1 \times 8 =$ _____

31. $9 \times 9 =$ _____ 32. $9 \times 7 =$ _____ 33. $9 \times 5 =$ _____ 34. $9 \times 6 =$ _____ 35. $9 \times 8 =$ _____

36. $7 \times 9 =$ _____ 37. $4 \times 9 =$ _____ 38. $2 \times 9 =$ _____ 39. $3 \times 9 =$ _____ 40. $6 \times 9 =$ _____

Word Problem

Draw a model and write a mathematical expression to represent the problem.
Then calculate and answer the question.

41. Ms. Park wants to divide her class of 28 students into 7 equal groups to work on a science project. How many students will be in each group? _____

   Model:

   Mathematical Expression:

Challenge Yourself

42. $20 \div 2 =$ _____ 43. $60 \div 3 =$ _____ 44. $8 \div 2 \div 2 =$ _____ 45. $27 \div 3 \div 3 =$ _____

2-11   Why is multiplying by 10 so easy?

Mathematical Conversation

We have already learned the multiplication tables for 2 through 9.

I wonder what the times table for 10 would look like. We had three lines for the 7 times table, two lines for the 8 times table, and only one line for the 9 times table. So I guess we will have no lines for the times table for ten.

You are probably right, Danny! We may not need a table for 10. Think about how many students there are in 3 groups with 10 students in each group. Can you solve the problem without a new times table?

That's 30 students! 3 × 10 = 30.

How about 3 groups with 20 students in each group? Hmm . . . There will be 60 students! 3 × 20 = 60.

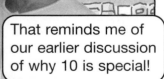

To multiply a number by 10, put a zero on the end of the number. To multiply a number by a multiple of ten, you multiply that number by the digit in the tens place and then put a zero at the end of the product.

That reminds me of our earlier discussion of why 10 is special!

Guided Practice

Try these on your own and fill in the answers.

A. 20 × 2 = _____   B. 30 × 3 = _____   C. 30 ÷ 3 = _____   D. 40 ÷ 2 = _____

Lesson 2–11 Exercises

Recite the multiplication tables from 2 to 9. Calculate these in your mind and fill in the answers.

1. $20 \times 3 =$ _____   2. $10 \times 6 =$ _____   3. $30 \times 3 =$ _____   4. $20 \times 4 =$ _____

5. $3 \times 20 =$ _____   6. $6 \times 10 =$ _____   7. $3 \times 30 =$ _____   8. $4 \times 20 =$ _____

9. $30 \div 3 =$ _____   10. $40 \div 2 =$ _____   11. $50 \div 5 =$ _____   12. $60 \div 6 =$ _____

13. $20 \div 2 =$ _____   14. $60 \div 2 =$ _____   15. $70 \div 7 =$ _____   16. $100 \div 5 =$ _____

17. $7 \times 3 =$ _____   18. $6 \times 6 =$ _____   19. $9 \times 5 =$ _____   20. $7 \times 7 =$ _____

21. $8 \times 6 =$ _____   22. $8 \times 7 =$ _____   23. $5 \times 9 =$ _____   24. $8 \times 8 =$ _____

25. $35 \div 5 =$ _____   26. $14 \div 7 =$ _____   27. $36 \div 9 =$ _____   28. $30 \div 6 =$ _____

29. $42 \div 7 =$ _____   30. $42 \div 6 =$ _____   31. $54 \div 6 =$ _____   32. $72 \div 8 =$ _____

33. $50 \times 2 =$ _____   34. $50 \times 3 =$ _____   35. $40 \times 3 =$ _____   36. $30 \times 6 =$ _____

37. $100 \div 2 =$ _____   38. $150 \div 3 =$ _____   39. $120 \div 3 =$ _____   40. $180 \div 3 =$ _____

41. $3 + 7 + 5 =$ _____   42. $9 + 3 + 1 =$ _____   43. $20 - 10 - 2 =$ _____   44. $30 - 7 - 6 =$ _____

45. $9 + 9 - 7 =$ _____   46. $15 - 5 + 9 =$ _____   47. $18 + 2 - 3 =$ _____   48. $32 - 3 + 4 =$ _____

Word Problems

Write a mathematical expression to solve each problem. Use the models to help you.

49. April, June, and September each have 30 days. How many days do the 3 months have altogether?

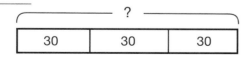

Mathematical expression:

50. If 30 apples are shared equally among 3 people, how many apples will each person receive? _____

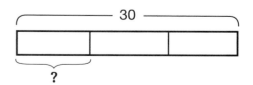

Mathematical expression:

Reflection and Discussion

Since you know that $20 \times 2 = 40$, how can you calculate 20×20?

51

2-12   Can you calculate 21 × 3?

Mathematical Conversation

Look! I filled up 21 rows of my stamp album. Each row holds 3 stamps. How many stamps do I have in my stamp album?

$21 \times 3 = 63$. I can't believe that I can do multiplication with a 2-digit number without pencil and paper!

You can probably do multiplication with a 3-digit number, too. Try this: $120 \times 2 = ?$

240!

Cool! I think I can do that, too!

Good for you!

Guided Practice

Try these on your own.

A. $13 \times 2 =$ ____   **B.** $22 \times 3 =$ ____   **C.** $33 \div 3 =$ ____   **D.** $84 \div 2 =$ ____

52

Lesson 2–12 Exercises

Recite the multiplication tables from 2 to 9. Calculate these in your mind and fill in the answers.

1. $12 \times 3 =$ _____   2. $22 \times 2 =$ _____   3. $31 \times 3 =$ _____   4. $34 \times 2 =$ _____

5. $12 \times 4 =$ _____   6. $22 \times 4 =$ _____   7. $21 \times 3 =$ _____   8. $42 \times 2 =$ _____

9. $39 \div 3 =$ _____   10. $44 \div 2 =$ _____   11. $55 \div 5 =$ _____   12. $63 \div 3 =$ _____

13. $86 \div 2 =$ _____   14. $66 \div 3 =$ _____   15. $77 \div 7 =$ _____   16. $28 \div 2 =$ _____

17. $4 \times 7 =$ _____   18. $5 \times 5 =$ _____   19. $9 \times 4 =$ _____   20. $7 \times 9 =$ _____

21. $8 \times 5 =$ _____   22. $8 \times 3 =$ _____   23. $6 \times 9 =$ _____   24. $3 \times 9 =$ _____

25. $20 \div 5 =$ _____   26. $21 \div 7 =$ _____   27. $36 \div 9 =$ _____   28. $16 \div 4 =$ _____

29. $14 \div 7 =$ _____   30. $40 \div 5 =$ _____   31. $36 \div 6 =$ _____   32. $16 \div 8 =$ _____

33. $60 \times 2 =$ _____   34. $40 \times 4 =$ _____   35. $30 \times 7 =$ _____   36. $60 \times 6 =$ _____

37. $100 \div 5 =$ _____   38. $150 \div 3 =$ _____   39. $120 \div 3 =$ _____   40. $180 \div 6 =$ _____

41. $5 + 7 + 5 =$ ___   42. $12 + 3 + 1 =$ ___   43. $35 - 4 - 1 =$ ___   44. $48 - 5 - 8 =$ ___

45. $12 + 8 - 8 =$ ___   46. $24 - 5 + 6 =$ ___   47. $40 + 4 - 6 =$ ___   48. $77 - 7 + 9 =$ ___

Word Problems

Write a mathematical expression to solve each problem. Use the models to help you.

49. January, March, and July each have 31 days. How many days do the 3 months have altogether? _____

?		
31	31	31

Mathematical expression:

50. A big box contains 48 tennis balls. A small box contains a dozen (12) balls. How many small boxes are there in a large box? _____

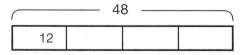

Mathematical expression:

Reflection and Discussion

Can you calculate $84 \div 21$ without using paper and pencil or a calculator?

2-13   Multiplication and division vs. addition and subtraction . . .

I understand what you've written except for one word. Addition and subtraction are inverses of each other. So are multiplication and division. But why does this say multiplication and division versus addition and subtraction?

**Multiplication and Division
versus
Addition and Subtraction**

I can't figure it out either.

Well, when we do a computation, multiplication and division take priority over addition and subtraction. For example, when calculating $3 + 2 \times 4$, we do 2×4 first. Then we add the product, 8, to 3. The result is 11.

Hmm . . . The rule isn't hard, but why do the operations get different priorities? Isn't it easier if we just compute from left to right?

As you learn more math, you will see that this rule makes complicated operations much easier.

Guided Practice

Try these on your own.

A. $3 + 3 \times 2 = $ ____   **B.** $10 + 5 \times 3 = $ ____   **C.** $15 + 3 \div 3 = $ ____   **D.** $28 - 25 \div 5 = $ ____

Lesson 2–13 Exercises

Recite the multiplication tables from 2 to 9. Calculate these in your mind and fill in the answers.

1. $4 \times 3 + 8 =$ ___
2. $5 \times 5 + 5 =$ ___
3. $7 \times 7 + 1 =$ ___
4. $3 \times 8 + 4 =$ ___

5. $8 + 4 \times 3 =$ ___
6. $5 + 5 \times 5 =$ ___
7. $1 + 7 \times 7 =$ ___
8. $4 + 3 \times 8 =$ ___

9. $7 \times 2 - 2 =$ ___
10. $15 \div 5 - 1 =$ ___
11. $40 \div 8 - 4 =$ ___
12. $8 \times 8 + 4 =$ ___

13. $7 - 2 \times 2 =$ ___
14. $15 - 5 \div 1 =$ ___
15. $40 - 8 \div 4 =$ ___
16. $8 + 8 \times 4 =$ ___

17. $2 \times 7 \div 2 =$ ___
18. $5 \times 6 \div 3 =$ ___
19. $9 \times 2 \div 6 =$ ___
20. $4 \times 6 \div 3 =$ ___

21. $8 \div 4 \times 8 =$ ___
22. $9 \div 3 \times 6 =$ ___
23. $6 \div 2 \times 5 =$ ___
24. $16 \div 2 \times 5 =$ ___

25. $7 + 7 - 4 =$ ___
26. $20 + 20 - 2 =$ ___
27. $8 + 7 - 6 =$ ___
28. $18 + 2 - 5 =$ ___

29. $9 - 7 + 2 =$ ___
30. $12 - 10 + 6 =$ ___
31. $8 - 7 + 6 =$ ___
32. $12 - 6 + 7 =$ ___

Word Problems

Write a mathematical expression to solve each problem. Use the models to help you.

33. A box contains 40 erasers in five different colors. There are the same number of erasers in each color. How many erasers of each color are there? _____

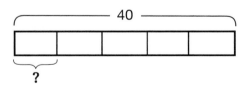

Mathematical expression:

34. A box contains 40 erasers. There are 8 erasers of each color. How many different colors are there?

_____

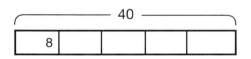

Mathematical expression:

Reflection and Discussion

Both word problems on this page use the same three numbers: 5, 8, and 40. Make up another word problem that uses these three numbers. You may write a division problem or a multiplication problem.

55

2-14   Unit 2 Review

Mathematical Conversation

Lesson 2–14 Exercises

Fill in this multiplication table.

2 × 2 =	2 × 3 =	2 × 4 =	2 × 5 =	2 × 6 =	2 × 7 =	2 × 8 =	2 × 9 =
3 × 2 =	3 × 3 =	3 × 4 =	3 × 5 =	3 × 6 =	3 × 7 =	3 × 8 =	3 × 9 =
4 × 2 =	4 × 3 =	4 × 4 =	4 × 5 =	4 × 6 =	4 × 7 =	4 × 8 =	4 × 9 =
5 × 2 =	5 × 3 =	5 × 4 =	5 × 5 =	5 × 6 =	5 × 7 =	5 × 8 =	5 × 9 =
6 × 2 =	6 × 3 =	6 × 4 =	6 × 5 =	6 × 6 =	6 × 7 =	6 × 8 =	6 × 9 =
7 × 2 =	7 × 3 =	7 × 4 =	7 × 5 =	7 × 6 =	7 × 7 =	7 × 8 =	7 × 9 =
8 × 2 =	8 × 3 =	8 × 4 =	8 × 5 =	8 × 6 =	8 × 7 =	8 × 8 =	8 × 9 =
9 × 2 =	9 × 3 =	9 × 4 =	9 × 5 =	9 × 6 =	9 × 7 =	9 × 8 =	9 × 9 =

Calculate and fill in the answers.

10 ÷ 2 = _____

20 ÷ 4 = _____   24 ÷ 4 = _____

30 ÷ 5 = _____   36 ÷ 6 = _____   40 ÷ 5 = _____

21 ÷ 7 = _____   16 ÷ 4 = _____   24 ÷ 8 = _____   12 ÷ 6 = _____

18 ÷ 3 = _____   14 ÷ 2 = _____   15 ÷ 3 = _____

18 ÷ 9 = _____   45 ÷ 9 = _____

25 ÷ 5 = _____

3-1 Why does "place" have a value?

Mathematical Conversation

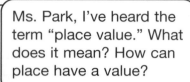

Ms. Park, I've heard the term "place value." What does it mean? How can place have a value?

Take a look at these cartoons. They will give you an answer.

Who can count faster?

1, 2, 3, 4, 5, 6, 7, 8, 9, 10

1, 2, 3, 4, 5, 6, 7, 8, 9, 10

1, 2, 3, 4, 5, 6, 7

. . .21, 22, 23

10, 20, 30, 40, 50, 60, 70, 80, 90, 100!

. . .72, 73, 74

I know why the girl on the left won. She made groups of 10 so that the big pile was easier to manage!

This idea started long ago, in ancient history. When people had to count many objects, they grouped the objects. People have 10 fingers, so the size of groups was often 10.

I see! So when they recorded the amount, I bet they put the number of groups next to the number of single pieces! That's how each place in a number got a different value! Of course, a group of 10 apples has a greater value than just one apple!

Do you remember that 10 is the special organizer of our numeral system?

Of course I do!

58

Lesson 3–1 Exercises

Rewrite these expressions in columns. Use place value to line up the numbers.
Then calculate and fill in the answers.

1. $3,200 + 32 =$ _____

2. $2,500 + 25 =$ _____

3. $71 + 7,100 =$ _____

4. $16 + 1,600 =$ _____

5. $3,200 + 320 =$ _____

6. $2,500 + 250 =$ _____

7. $710 + 7,100 =$ _____

8. $160 + 1,600 =$ _____

9. $8,585 - 32 =$ _____

10. $5,555 - 14 =$ _____

11. $9,500 - 400 =$ _____

12. $7,840 - 320 =$ _____

13. $8,585 - 320 =$ _____

14. $5,555 - 140 =$ _____

15. $9,500 - 4,000 =$ _____

16. $7,840 - 3,200 =$ _____

Calculate these in your mind and fill in the answers.

17. $33 \times 2 =$ _____

18. $40 \times 4 =$ _____

19. $50 \times 5 =$ _____

20. $60 \times 6 =$ _____

21. $80 \div 2 =$ _____

22. $120 \div 3 =$ _____

23. $240 \div 8 =$ _____

24. $280 \div 7 =$ _____

25. $4 + 7 + 3 =$ _____

26. $20 - 6 - 4 =$ _____

27. $15 - 5 + 5 =$ _____

28. $52 - 3 + 4 =$ _____

Word Problems

Draw a model and write a mathematical expression to represent these problems.
Then calculate and answer the questions.

29. Ms. Park packed 50 bottles equally into 5 boxes. How many bottles did she pack in each box? _____

Model:

Mathematical expression:

30. Last week Danny recycled 30 cans. Ana recycled 42 cans. How many cans did they recycle? _____

Model:

Mathematical expression:

Reflection and Discussion   Do you think it is a good idea to have 10 as a special organizer in our numeral system? Why? Are there times when other numbers are used as organizers?

3-2   What happens when you go right?

Mathematical Conversation

Please read this number. There are 7 ones in the number. Each has a different value according to its place. Do you see a pattern?

Hey, I see a pattern. As you move to the left, the value of each place is 10 times the value of the place before. See, the ones place is 10 times the tenths place; the tens place is 10 times the ones place.

There's a pattern when you move to the right as well.

See, I told you. 10 really is a special organizer.

thousands (10 × 100) 10 hundreds	hundreds (10 × 10) ten tens	tens (10 × 1) 10 ones	ones (10 × 0.1) ten tenths	tenths (10 × 0.01) ten hundredths	hundredths (10 × 0.001) 10 thousandths	thousandths
1,	1	1	1 .	1	1	1

Guided Practice

Rewrite these expressions in columns. Then calculate and fill in the answers.

A. 345.9 − 23.5 = ____   B. 527 + 6.05 = ____

Fill in the blanks with >, <, or =.

C.   1 ____ 0.999   D. 1.2 ____ 2.1

E. 1.03 ____ 1.003   F. 9.7 ____ 9.7

Lesson 3-2 Exercises

Rewrite these expressions in columns. Use place value to line up the numbers. Then calculate and fill in the answers.

1. $1.2 + 3.5 =$ _____
2. $6.4 + 0.3 =$ _____
3. $7.1 + 1.8 =$ _____
4. $1.6 + 5.2 =$ _____

5. $12.5 + 2.4 =$ _____
6. $3.3 + 33.3 =$ _____
7. $45.6 + 0.22 =$ _____
8. $20 + 0.2 =$ _____

9. $4.5 - 3.2 =$ _____
10. $5.56 - 1.42 =$ _____
11. $95.6 - 12 =$ _____
12. $0.4 - 0.2 =$ _____

13. $8.5 - 1.1 =$ _____
14. $54.8 - 2.5 =$ _____
15. $188.9 - 52 =$ _____
16. $7.84 - 0.4 =$ _____

Calculate these in your mind and fill in the answers.

17. $27 + 8 =$ _____
18. $66 + 6 =$ _____
19. $86 + 5 =$ _____
20. $48 + 8 =$ _____

21. $32 - 5 =$ _____
22. $74 - 5 =$ _____
23. $55 - 8 =$ _____
24. $81 - 7 =$ _____

25. $5 + 6 + 5 =$ _____
26. $40 - 8 - 2 =$ _____
27. $24 - 8 + 7 =$ _____
28. $35 - 6 + 7 =$ _____

Fill in the blanks with $>$, $<$, or $=$.

29. 1 _____ 1.1
30. 9.5 _____ 9.05
31. 18.8 _____ 188
32. 0.004 _____ 0.0005

Word Problems

Draw models and write mathematical expressions to represent these problems. Then calculate and answer the questions.

33. Danny bought 5.6 pounds of apples and 1.2 pounds of oranges. How many pounds of fruit did Danny buy? _____ _____

Model:

Mathematical expression:

34. Ana needs 2.5 cups of white flour and 1.5 cups of rye to make bread. How much more white than rye does she need? _____ _____

Model:

Mathematical expression:

Reflection and Discussion To decide how great a number is, which is more important to know: where the digits are placed, or what the digits are?

3-3   Where should I put the 1?

Mathematical Conversation

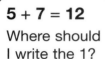

5 + 7 = 12
Where should I write the 1?

If you use the real names for numbers, it's easy! The 1 means 1 ten, so you can put it in the tens column. You "store" the 1 near the 2, then add it when you work in the tens column.

OK. Then I get 4 in the tens place and 7 in the hundreds place.

625 + 117 =

625
+ 117

625 + 117 = 742

  1
 625
+ 117
 742

Let me change one digit in the problem to make it more challenging.

I bet this time we have to store a 1 in the hundreds column.

So this time the 1 is 1 hundred.

625 + 187 =

1 1
625
+ 187

Look at the change I made. Can you calculate this?

62.5 + 18.7 = ?

Guided Practice

Rewrite these expressions in columns. Then calculate and fill in the answers.

A. 355 + 126 = ____   B. 473 + 272 = ____   C. 56.2 + 1.9 = ____   D. 341.8 + 100.4 = ____

Lesson 3–3 Exercises

Rewrite these problems in columns. Use place value to line up the numbers.
Then calculate and fill in the answers.

1. $36 + 25 =$ _____   **2.** $456 + 216 =$ _____   **3.** $877 + 415 =$ _____   **4.** $122 + 78 =$ _____

5. $77 + 14 =$ _____   **6.** $738 + 181 =$ _____   **7.** $433 + 286 =$ _____   **8.** $345 + 165 =$ _____

9. $7.5 + 2.6 =$ ___   **10.** $0.17 + 0.05 =$ ___   **11.** $8.36 + 1.16 =$ ___   **12.** $4.55 + 2.17 =$ ___

13. $3,006 + 179 =$ ___   **14.** $1,368 + 2,581 =$ ___   **15.** $7,182 + 2,047 =$ ___   **16.** $30.06 + 1.79 =$ ___

Calculate these in your mind and fill in the answers.

17. $123 \times 3 =$ _____   **18.** $400 \times 4 =$ _____   **19.** $60 \times 5 =$ _____   **20.** $70 \times 6 =$ _____

21. $100 \div 2 =$ _____   **22.** $160 \div 4 =$ _____   **23.** $240 \div 6 =$ _____   **24.** $350 \div 7 =$ _____

25. $3 + 3 + 3 =$ _____   **26.** $5 + 5 + 5 =$ _____   **27.** $4 + 4 + 4 =$ _____   **28.** $2 + 2 + 2 =$ _____

29. $9 + 9 + 9 =$ _____   **30.** $6 + 6 + 6 =$ _____   **31.** $7 + 7 + 7 =$ _____   **32.** $8 + 8 + 8 =$ _____

Word Problems

Draw a model and write a mathematical expression to represent these problems.
Then calculate and answer the questions.

33. The school is 1.5 miles north of Danny's home. The library is 2.7 miles north of the school. How many miles north of Danny's home is the library? _____

Model:

Mathematical expression:

34. Ana spent 0.5 hour doing math homework and 0.8 hour doing English homework. How many hours did she spend on homework? _____

Model:

Mathematical expression:

Reflection and Discussion

Without doing the problems, decide which calculation would be easier: 3.5 + 0.6 or 3.5 + 0.06. Why is it easier?

3-4 Help! There aren't enough ones to do subtraction!

Mathematical Conversation

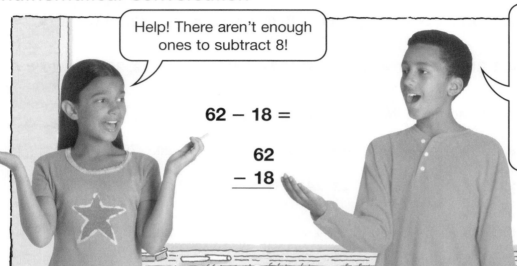

Help! There aren't enough ones to subtract 8!

$62 - 18 =$

$$\begin{array}{r} 62 \\ - 18 \\ \hline \end{array}$$

Wait a minute! In the last lesson, when we added and had too many ones, we composed a ten. Why don't you decompose one of the tens? That will give you 12 ones. You can subtract 8 from 12.

Good idea! Thank you! So I have $12 - 8$ equals 4, and 5 tens $-$ 1 ten equals 4 tens. Then I get 44.

$62 - 18 = 44$

$$\begin{array}{r} \overset{5\ 12}{\cancel{62}} \\ - 18 \\ \hline 44 \end{array}$$

Actually, I know some other ways to do that computation.

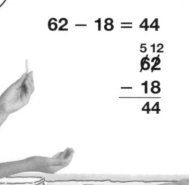

I know other ways to regroup, too!

Really?

Guided Practice

Rewrite these expressions in columns. Then calculate and fill in the answers.

A. $355 - 126 =$ ____   **B.** $423 - 262 =$ ____   **C.** $56.2 - 1.9 =$ ____   **D.** $341.1 - 200.3 =$ ____

Lesson 3–4 Exercises

Rewrite these expressions in columns. Line up the numbers carefully.
Then calculate and fill in the answers.

1. $184 - 75 =$ _____

2. $984 - 335 =$ _____

3. $450 - 255 =$ _____

4. $333 - 206 =$ _____

5. $549 - 146 =$ _____

6. $832 - 7 =$ _____

7. $453 - 146 =$ _____

8. $218 - 120 =$ _____

9. $3.5 - 1.7 =$ _____

10. $55.7 - 18.2 =$ _____

11. $8.3 - 1.6 =$ _____

12. $3.22 - 0.6 =$ _____

13. $8.8 - 6.9 =$ _____

14. $1.2 - 0.8 =$ _____

15. $12.8 - 1.9 =$ _____

16. $1.4 - 1.7 =$ _____

17. $2,340 - 1,006 =$ _____

18. $4,928 - 1,845 =$ _____

19. $6,694 - 2,275 =$ _____

Calculate these in your mind and fill in the answers.

20. $8 + 6 =$ _____

21. $7 + 8 =$ _____

22. $5 + 8 =$ _____

23. $6 + 8 =$ _____

24. $13 - 5 =$ _____

25. $15 - 7 =$ _____

26. $12 - 5 =$ _____

27. $13 - 8 =$ _____

28. $18 - 4 - 4 =$ _____

29. $19 - 4 - 5 =$ _____

30. $28 - 2 - 6 =$ _____

31. $59 - 6 - 3 =$ _____

32. $16 - 5 - 1 =$ _____

33. $17 - 6 - 1 =$ _____

34. $74 - 2 - 12 =$ _____

35. $87 - 3 - 4 =$ _____

Word Problems

Draw models and write mathematical expressions to represent these problems.
Then calculate and answer the questions.

36. Maria spent 3.5 hours reading two books. Reading the first book took 2.6 hours. How long did the second book take? _____

Model:

Mathematical expression:

37. An elephant is 3.2 meters high. A camel is 1.7 meters high. How much higher is the elephant than the camel? _____

Model:

Mathematical expression:

Reflection and Discussion

How would you calculate $1 - 0.0001$?

3-5   Review, Reflection, and Quiz 5

Mathematical Conversation

Quiz 5

Calculate and fill in the answers. Rewrite in columns if you need to.

1. $104 + 75 = $ _____
2. $623 + 4 = $ _____
3. $984 + 12 = $ _____
4. $456 + 225 = $ _____

5. $813 + 209 = $ _____
6. $368 + 29 = $ _____
7. $584 - 222 = $ _____
8. $458 - 230 = $ _____

9. $854 - 312 = $ _____
10. $430 - 205 = $ _____
11. $956 - 207 = $ _____
12. $512 - 104 = $ _____

13. $32.7 + 44.2 = $ _____
14. $4.3 + 1.8 = $ _____
15. $7.12 + 0.6 = $ _____
16. $3.6 - 0.7 = $ _____

17. $8.8 - 0.3 = $ _____
18. $7.5 - 0.9 = $ _____
19. $12.8 - 2.7 = $ _____
20. $1.2 - 0.6 = $ _____

Fill in the blanks with >, <, or =.

21. 1 _____ 0.1
22. 6.4 _____ 6.04
23. 232 _____ 332
24. 0.001 _____ 0.0009

Word Problem

Draw a model and write a mathematical expression to represent this problem.
Then calculate and answer the question.

25. Derek took 0.3 hour to do the first part of a math quiz and 0.7 hour to do the rest. How many hours did Derek take to finish the whole quiz? _____

Model:

Mathematical expression:

Challenge Yourself

26. $2,250 + 21 = $ _____
27. $3,773 + 23 = $ _____
28. $4,510 + 104 = $ _____
29. $421.5 + 23.4 = $ _____

3-6   If you know how 312 x 3 works, then . . .

Mathematical Conversation

Here is one way to calculate 312 x 3. Do you know how it works?

I know! We multiply each digit in 312 by 3. Start from the ones place of 312: 3 times 2 is 6; that's 6 ones. Next, 3 times 1 is 3; that's 3 tens. Then we multiply 3 times 3 to get 9 hundreds.

```
  312
×   3
  936
```

Multiplication with a 4-digit number works the same way.

That's right. Place value is very important when we work with multidigit numbers.

3,124 × 2 = 6,248

```
3,124
 ×  2
6,248
```

This is really cool!

Guided Practice

Rewrite these expressions in columns. Then calculate and fill in the answers.

A. 434 × 2 = _____   **B.** 3,323 × 2 = _____   **C.** 232 × 3 = _____   **D.** 2,212 × 4 = _____

68

Lesson 3–6 Exercises

Rewrite these expressions in columns. Then calculate and fill in the answers. Check your answers with a calculator.

1. $121 \times 2 = $ _____

2. $323 \times 3 = $ _____

3. $422 \times 4 = $ _____

4. $333 \times 2 = $ _____

5. $121 \times 4 = $ _____

6. $323 \times 2 = $ _____

7. $222 \times 3 = $ _____

8. $333 \times 3 = $ _____

9. $122 \times 3 = $ _____

10. $1.22 \times 3 = $ _____

11. $1{,}220 \times 3 = $ _____

12. $22 \times 3 = $ _____

13. $12.2 \times 3 = $ _____

14. $0.122 \times 3 = $ _____

15. $12{,}200 \times 3 = $ _____

16. $2.2 \times 3 = $ _____

Calculate these in your mind and fill in the answers.

17. $56 + 14 = $ _____

18. $38 + 6 = $ _____

19. $17 + 18 = $ _____

20. $25 + 26 = $ _____

21. $80 - 2 = $ _____

22. $60 - 5 = $ _____

23. $50 - 8 = $ _____

24. $100 - 9 = $ _____

25. $15 + 15 + 5 = $ _____

26. $23 + 23 + 4 = $ _____

27. $77 - 2 - 7 = $ _____

28. $86 - 4 - 6 = $ _____

29. $30 + 30 - 30 = $ _____

30. $60 - 5 + 15 = $ _____

31. $58 + 2 - 8 = $ _____

32. $44 - 14 + 4 = $ _____

Word Problems

Draw a model and write a mathematical expression to represent these problems. Then calculate and answer the questions.

33. A large bag of rice contains 12 pounds. C.J.'s mom bought 3 bags. How much rice did she buy?

   _____

   Model:

   Mathematical expression:

34. Two buses can carry 84 people. If each bus can carry the same number of people, how many people can each bus carry?

   _____

   Model:

   Mathematical expression:

Reflection and Discussion

Can you calculate 821×4? (Bonus problem)

3-7   Where will the bonus problem lead us?

Mathematical Conversation

This is the bonus problem you had yesterday. Do you know why it's a bonus problem?

821 × 4 = 3,284

$$\begin{array}{r} 821 \\ \times\ 4 \\ \hline 3,284 \end{array}$$

Look at the hundreds place! When you calculate 8 x 4, you get 32, which is a 2-digit number.

Now let me make a small change. I will switch the 8 in the hundreds place with the 2 in the tens place. Will you still be able to find a place to write the 32?

Let's see, 32 tens . . . I know! We can do what we did with addition. We can store the 3 above the hundreds place, and then add it to the product of 4 times 2.

Good idea, Ana.

We can use what we already know to help us learn new things!

281 × 4 =

$$\begin{array}{r} 3 \\ 281 \\ \times\ 4 \\ \hline 1,124 \end{array}$$

Wow! this time they stored a 3!

Guided Practice

Rewrite these expressions in columns. Then calculate and fill in the answers.

A. 124 × 4 = ____   **B.** 321 × 6 = ____   **C.** 542 × 3 = ____   **D.** 2,232 × 4 = ____

Lesson 3-7 Exercises

Rewrite these expressions in columns. Then calculate and fill in the answers.

1. $332 \times 4 =$ _____

2. $5\,61 \times 7 =$ _____

3. $332 \times 2 =$ _____

4. $5,611 \times 7 =$ _____

5. $242 \times 8 =$ _____

6. $333 \times 9 =$ _____

7. $242 \times 4 =$ _____

8. $313 \times 9 =$ _____

9. $715 \times 3 =$ _____

10. $352 \times 8 =$ _____

11. $533 \times 4 =$ _____

12. $333 \times 2 =$ _____

Calculate these in your mind and fill in answers.

13. $65 + 20 =$ _____

14. $34 + 8 =$ _____

15. $25 + 7 =$ _____

16. $18 + 26 =$ _____

17. $90 - 9 =$ _____

18. $80 - 8 =$ _____

19. $70 - 7 =$ _____

20. $100 - 1 =$ _____

21. $45 + 5 + 45 =$ _____

22. $26 + 18 + 4 =$ _____

23. $34 - 2 - 3 =$ _____

24. $73 - 6 - 3 =$ _____

25. $24 + 68 - 68 =$ _____

26. $92 - 12 + 15 =$ _____

27. $89 + 9 - 8 =$ _____

28. $54 + 9 - 4 =$ _____

Word Problems

Draw a model and write a mathematical expression to represent these problems. Then calculate and answer the questions.

29. The 9 classes in C.J.'s school donated books to the school library. Each class donated 35 books. How many library books were donated?

_____

Model:

Mathematical expression:

30. For a paper folding project, 9 children made paper cranes. Each child made 12 cranes. How many cranes did the children make?

_____

Model:

Mathematical expression:

Reflection and Discussion

Compare the across-ten addition in 214×7 and $214 + 7$. Is the across-ten addition in multiplication like that in addition?

3-8   Hey, there's a zero in between!

Mathematical Conversation

Do you see anything special about this computation?

Well, there's a 0 between the hundreds place and the ones place.

$405 \times 9 =$

$$\begin{array}{r} 405 \\ \times\ 9 \\ \hline 3{,}645 \end{array}$$

Let me do it! . . .

Look at this Danny. It's easier than the 3-digit multiplication we did before.

How about this one?

$4{,}005 \times 9 =$

$$\begin{array}{r} 4{,}005 \\ \times\ 9 \\ \hline 36{,}045 \end{array}$$

I need a 0 in the hundreds place.

Guided Practice

Rewrite these expressions in columns. Then calculate and fill in the answers.

A. 203 × 6 = _____   **B.** 102 × 4 = _____   **c.** 1,002 × 3 = _____   **D.** 2,005 × 7 = _____

Lesson 3–8 Exercises

Rewrite these expressions in columns. Then calculate and fill in the answers.

1. $203 \times 3 = $ _____   **2.** $703 \times 5 = $ _____   **3.** $804 \times 3 = $ _____   **4.** $804 \times 6 = $ _____

5. $126 \times 6 = $ _____   **6.** $202 \times 8 = $ _____   **7.** $805 \times 7 = $ _____   **8.** $303 \times 3 = $ _____

9. $126 \times 3 = $ _____   **10.** $202 \times 4 = $ _____   **11.** $805 \times 3 = $ _____   **12.** $303 \times 9 = $ _____

Calculate these in your mind and fill in the answers.

13. $36 + 20 = $ _____   **14.** $46 + 8 = $ _____   **15.** $75 + 5 = $ _____   **16.** $28 + 22 = $ _____

17. $80 - 7 = $ _____   **18.** $70 - 9 = $ _____   **19.** $61 - 7 = $ _____   **20.** $100 - 6 = $ _____

21. $28 + 15 + 2 = $ _____   **22.** $26 + 35 + 5 = $ _____   **23.** $21 - 9 - 1 = $ _____   **24.** $64 - 6 - 4 = $ _____

25. $42 + 8 - 2 = $ _____   **26.** $70 - 52 + 52 = $ _____   **27.** $91 + 9 - 1 = $ _____   **28.** $32 + 4 + 4 = $ _____

Word Problems

**Draw a model and write a mathematical expression to represent these problems.
Then calculate and answer the questions.**

29. Danny keeps 201 baseball cards in each box. If he has 4 boxes of cards, how many cards does he have? _____

Model:

Mathematical expression:

30. Ana collected 103 leaves for a mural and C.J. collected 105 leaves. How many leaves did Ana and C.J. collect? _____

Model:

Mathematical expression:

Reflection and Discussion

Can you calculate 603×3 in your head?

73

3-9   Unit 3 Review

Mathematical Conversation

Yes, tomorrow is the last day for this unit.

Ms. Park, we will have a test tomorrow, right?

I am very proud of myself. Now I can do advanced calculations. I can calculate with multidigit numbers and with decimals!

I have a challenge for you. Can you fill in the blanks? Here is a hint: You may need to use decimals for some of these.

1,295 = _____ tenths

1,295 = _____ ones

1,295 = _____ tens

1,295 = _____ hundreds

1,295 = _____ thousands

That's five ways to think about the same number!

74

Lesson 3-9 Exercises

Fill in the blanks with >, <, or =.

1. 4,120 _____ 3,900   2. 10 _____ 101   3. 403 _____ 304

4.   1.2 _____ 2   5. 0.5 _____ 0.07   6. 10.8 _____ 1.08

Calculate and fill in the answers. Rewrite in columns if you need to.

7. $761 + 127 =$ _____   8. $404 + 175 =$ _____

9. $1{,}623 + 3{,}405 =$ _____   10. $8.13 + 10.6 =$ _____

11. $3.6 + 3.09 =$ _____   12. $8.3 + 0.7 =$ _____

13. $983 - 143 =$ _____   14. $184 - 15 =$ _____

15. $8{,}854 - 5{,}312 =$ _____   16. $4.13 - 2.02 =$ _____

17. $51.24 - 1.12 =$ _____   18. $0.43 - 0.24 =$ _____

19. $412 \times 2 =$ _____   20. $131 \times 5 =$ _____

21. $432 \times 4 =$ _____   22. $712 \times 6 =$ _____

23. $82 \times 3 =$ _____   24. $25 \times 7 =$ _____

25. $112 \times 8 =$ _____

4-1   Letters in an equation?

Mathematical Conversation

Lily, do you understand this poster? Why are there letters in this equation?

Hmm . . . I think "l" stands for the length of the rectangle, and "w" stands for its width. "$l + l + w + w$" means add the two lengths and the two widths. But what does "P" mean?

l

w

$P = l + l + w + w$

"P" stands for perimeter. Perimeter is the distance around a shape. Does the equation make sense to you now?

I remember seeing letters in my sister's algebra book: $x + 8 = 10$. That's another equation with letters!

I think that equation means some number plus 8 equals 10.

Yes, you are right! In mathematics, "x" stands for an unknown number. As you learn more mathematics, you will find out more about the power of numbers.

Remember that "x" stands for an unknown number.

Got it!

Guided Practice

Find the number that x represents and fill in the answers.

A. $x + 5 = 15$ **B.** $20 − x = 17$ **C.** $x \times 4 = 24$ **D.** $42 \div x = 6$

$x =$ ____ $x =$ ____ $x =$ ____ $x =$ ____

Lesson 4–1 Exercises

Find the number that x represents and fill in the answers.

1. $x + 15 = 25$

   $x =$ ____

2. $70 - x = 60$

   $x =$ ____

3. $x \times 6 = 18$

   $x =$ ____

4. $35 \div x = 7$

   $x =$ ____

5. $28 + x = 37$

   $x =$ ____

6. $41 - 2 = x$

   $x =$ ____

7. $9 \times x = 27$

   $x =$ ____

8. $20 \div x = 5$

   $x =$ ____

9. $x + 7 = 42$

   $x =$ ____

10. $22 - x = 16$

    $x =$ ____

11. $x \times 5 = 40$

    $x =$ ____

12. $40 \div x = 10$

    $x =$ ____

13. $69 + x = 72$

    $x =$ ____

14. $35 - 6 = x$

    $x =$ ____

15. $7 \times x = 28$

    $x =$ ____

16. $49 \div x = 7$

    $x =$ ____

Calculate these in your mind and fill in the answers.

17. $36 + 6 =$ ____

18. $47 + 4 =$ ____

19. $15 + 15 =$ ____

20. $28 + 5 =$ ____

21. $80 - 9 =$ ____

22. $70 - 3 =$ ____

23. $61 - 8 =$ ____

24. $100 - 60 =$ ____

25. $17 + 9 =$ ____

26. $38 + 9 =$ ____

27. $23 + 9 =$ ____

28. $45 + 9 =$ ____

29. $17 - 9 =$ ____

30. $38 - 3 =$ ____

31. $23 - 8 =$ ____

32. $45 - 9 =$ ____

These equations use two letters. Find the number that x represents and fill in the answers.

33. $x + y = 32$

    and $y = 20$

    $x =$ ____

34. $x - y = 32$

    and $y = 2$

    $x =$ ____

35. $x \times y = 32$

    and $y = 4$

    $x =$ ____

36. $x \div y = 32$

    and $y = 2$

    $x =$ ____

Reflection and Discussion

If $x + y = 10$, how many different pairs of x and y could there be? What are they? What happens if you include decimal numbers?

4-2   How can the Commutative Law help?

Mathematical Conversation

Have you heard of the Commutative Law? These equations show what it means for addition and multiplication.

The Commutative Law has already helped us! Because $a + b = b + a$, we only needed to memorize half of the addition facts. Because $a \times b = b \times a$, we only needed to memorize half of the times tables!

$$a + b = b + a$$
$$a \times b = b \times a$$

Yes! If I know that $8 + 7 = 15$, then I know that $7 + 8 = 15$. If I know that $8 \times 7 = 56$, then I know that $7 \times 8 = 56$, too.

The Commutative Law also applies when we have more than two numbers. For example, the Commutative Law makes these calculations easier: $25 + 68 + 5$ and $5 \times 45 \times 2$.

And here's how it works for the multiplication problem.

I see! Here's how it works for the first one.

$$25 + 68 + 5 = 25 + 5 + 68$$
$$= 30 + 68$$
$$= 98$$

$$5 \times 45 \times 2 = 5 \times 2 \times 45$$
$$= 10 \times 45$$
$$= 450$$

Get ready for algebra!

No problem!

Guided Practice

Use the Commutative Law to do these calculations and fill in the answers.

A. $97 + 86 + 3 =$ _____

B. $50 + 38 + 50 =$ _____

C. $5 \times 86 \times 2 =$ _____

D. $2 \times 47 \times 50 =$ _____

Lesson 4–2 Exercises

Use the Commutative Law to help do these calculations and fill in the answers.

1. $199 + 85 + 1 =$ _____
2. $450 + 76 + 50 =$ _____
3. $80 + 90 + 20 =$ _____

4. $75 + 88 + 25 =$ _____
5. $26 + 48 + 24 =$ _____
6. $170 + 59 + 30 =$ _____

7. $2 \times 4 \times 5 =$ _____
8. $2 \times 9 \times 3 =$ _____
9. $3 \times 8 \times 3 =$ _____

10. $5 \times 7 \times 2 =$ _____
11. $50 \times 7 \times 2 =$ _____
12. $28 \times 9 \times 0 =$ _____

Use the Commutative Law to write another version of each mathematical expression.

13. $7 + 33 =$ _____
14. $6 + 78 =$ _____
15. $9 + 52 =$ _____
16. $22 + 29 =$ _____

17. $3 \times 7 =$ _____
18. $4 \times 9 =$ _____
19. $5 \times 8 =$ _____
20. $6 \times 100 =$ _____

Calculate these in your mind and fill in the answers.

21. $34 + 12 =$ _____
22. $58 + 4 =$ _____
23. $72 + 11 =$ _____
24. $45 + 45 =$ _____

25. $40 - 7 =$ _____
26. $34 - 5 =$ _____
27. $28 - 14 =$ _____
28. $60 - 9 =$ _____

29. $22 + 33 =$ _____
30. $69 + 8 =$ _____
31. $42 + 52 =$ _____
32. $37 + 6 =$ _____

33. $73 - 7 =$ _____
34. $84 - 9 =$ _____
35. $50 - 8 =$ _____
36. $25 - 6 =$ _____

Word Problems

Draw a model and write a mathematical expression to represent these problems.
Then calculate and answer the questions.

37. On a field trip, one adult is needed for every 4 students. How many adults are needed for a class of 24 students? _____

    Model:

    Mathematical expression:

38. On a field trip, one adult is needed for every 4 students. How many adults are needed for a class of 25 students? _____

    Model:

    Mathematical expression:

Reflection and Discussion

Calculate $198 + 85 + 2$ with and without using the Commutative Law. Which way is easier? Why?

4-3 What is the Associative Law?

Mathematical Conversation

We haven't talked about the Associative Law yet. You will like it, too.

You mean that if we're adding more than two numbers, we can group some numbers and add them together first? And this works for multiplication, too?

Associative Law of addition
$$a + b + c = a + (b + c)$$

Associative Law of multiplication
$$a \times b \times c = a \times (b \times c)$$

Yes!

$$a + b + c = a + (b + c) = b + c + a$$

I will try it for multiplication.

Let me try it for addition. It works!

$$4 + 3 + 2 = 4 + (3 + 2) \qquad 4 \times 3 \times 2 = 4 \times (3 \times 2)$$
$$= 4 + 5 \qquad\qquad\qquad = 4 \times 6$$
$$= 9 \qquad\qquad\qquad\qquad = 24$$

The Associative Law can also help with computation!

Wow!

Guided Practice

Use the Commutative and Associative Laws to do these calculations.

A. $53 + 88 + 12 =$ _____

B. $47 + 36 + 53 =$ _____

C. $24 \times 4 \times 5 =$ _____

D. $5 \times 62 \times 2 =$ _____

Lesson 4-3 Exercises

Make the following calculations using the Associative Law and fill in the answers.

1. $356 + 80 + 20 =$ ____

2. $278 + 70 + 30 =$ ____

3. $88 + 90 + 10 =$ ____

4. $75 + 8 + 2 =$ ____

5. $26 + 9 + 1 =$ ____

6. $177 + 5 + 5 =$ ____

7. $35 \times 5 \times 2 =$ ____

8. $94 \times 5 \times 2 =$ ____

9. $3 \times 50 \times 2 =$ ____

10. $67 \times 2 \times 5 =$ ____

11. $57 \times 2 \times 5 =$ ____

12. $14 \times 20 \times 5 =$ ____

Use the Associative Law to write another version of each mathematical expression.

13. $7 + 33 + 67 =$ _____

14. $6 + 78 + 22 =$ _____

15. $9 + 52 + 48 =$ _____

16. $15 \times 2 \times 5 =$ _____

17. $99 \times 5 \times 2 =$ _____

18. $27 \times 5 \times 2 =$ _____

Calculate these in your mind and fill in the answers.

19. $120 + 120 =$ ____

20. $230 + 230 =$ ____

21. $400 + 400 =$ ____

22. $420 + 420 =$ ____

23. $400 - 200 =$ ____

24. $340 - 40 =$ ____

25. $280 - 70 =$ ____

26. $600 - 90 =$ ____

27. $29 + 7 =$ ____

28. $96 + 5 =$ ____

29. $45 + 7 =$ ____

30. $73 + 8 =$ ____

31. $75 - 8 =$ ____

32. $83 - 5 =$ ____

33. $30 - 21 =$ ____

34. $45 - 6 =$ ____

Word Problems

Draw a model and write a mathematical expression to represent these problems. Then calculate and answer the questions.

35. Lily has 8 red marbles, 19 blue marbles, and 2 golden marbles. How many marbles does she have?

    _____

    Model:

    Mathematical expression:

36. Danny has 30 books on his bookshelf and 12 books on his desk. How many more books are there on his shelf than on his desk? _____

    Model:

    Mathematical expression:

Reflection and Discussion

Calculate $356 + 80 + 20$ with and without using the Associative Law. Which way is easier? Why?

4-4   Are there numbers less than 0?

Mathematical Conversation

I spent every penny to buy a present for my mom. Now I have 0 dollars. Nobody can have less money than I do.

I do! I had 5 dollars. My favorite car model costs 7 dollars. I borrowed 2 dollars from my brother to buy it. Now I owe him 2 dollars.

We say that Danny now has ⁻2 dollars. This means we are dealing with a negative number. A negative number is less than 0.

Tomorrow I will earn 2 dollars by mowing the lawn. I will return the 2 dollars to my brother. Then I will have 0 dollars—that's more than what I have now. If I can earn 3 dollars, then I will have 1 dollar, which is more than 0 dollars!

Danny, you just did a computation with negative numbers!

$$5 - 7 = {}^-2 \qquad 2 + ({}^-2) = 0 \qquad 3 + ({}^-2) = 1$$

What pattern do you see in these equations?

Guided Practice

Calculate and fill in the answers.

A. $3 + ({}^-3) =$ ____

B. $4 + ({}^-6) =$ ____

C. $3 - 10 =$ ____

D. $9 + ({}^-9) =$ ____

E. $6 + ({}^-4) =$ ____

F. $20 - 30 =$ ____

Lesson 4–4 Exercises

Calculate and fill in the answers.

1. $1 + (^-1) =$ ____

2. $5 + (^-5) =$ ____

3. $10 + (^-10) =$ ____

4. $12 + (^-12) =$ ____

5. $30 + (^-30) =$ ____

6. $100 + (^-100) =$ ____

7. $1 + (^-3) =$ ____

8. $5 + (^-7) =$ ____

9. $10 + (^-17) =$ ____

10. $12 + (^-14) =$ ____

11. $30 + (^-35) =$ ____

12. $100 + (^-102) =$ ____

13. $4 + (^-1) =$ ____

14. $15 + (^-5) =$ ____

15. $14 + (^-10) =$ ____

16. $14 + (^-12) =$ ____

17. $33 + (^-30) =$ ____

18. $105 + (^-100) =$ ____

19. $9 - 5 =$ ____

20. $12 - 8 =$ ____

21. $10 - 7 =$ ____

22. $12 - 4 =$ ____

23. $32 - 25 =$ ____

24. $100 - 5 =$ ____

25. $1 - 5 =$ ____

26. $9 - 10 =$ ____

27. $5 - 10 =$ ____

28. $2 - 4 =$ ____

29. $6 - 12 =$ ____

30. $2 - 100 =$ ____

31. $90 + (^-100) =$ ____

32. $230 + (^-250) =$ ____

33. $400 + (^-600) =$ ____

34. $200 - 400 =$ ____

35. $40 - 340 =$ ____

36. $10 - 270 =$ ____

37. $25 + 7 =$ ____

38. $96 + 6 =$ ____

39. $47 + 13 =$ ____

40. $84 - 8 =$ ____

41. $33 - 5 =$ ____

42. $80 - 72 =$ ____

Reflection and Discussion

Danny has no money. He borrowed 5 dollars from his sister and spent it all on lunch. How much money does he owe his sister? How much money does he have?

4-5   Unit 4 Review

Mathematical Conversation

In this unit, the equations with letters impressed me the most. They are different from what we have seen before.

Look at Danny's two examples carefully and tell me the differences between them.

I see two differences. First, there is a letter in the top one and there are only numbers in the bottom one. Second, the top one has something on both sides of the equals sign, and the bottom one has nothing after the equals sign.

$$3 + x = 5$$
$$3 + 2 =$$

Good, Lily. Equations can be written using letters to stand for unknown numbers. What else do you remember learning in this unit?

We learned about the Commutative and Associative Laws. But the Commutative Law was not totally new to us. We had used it before.

We also learned about negative numbers. They are cool!

Are negative numbers new to you?

Yup!

84

Lesson 4–5 Exercises

Find the number that x represents and fill in the answers.

1. $x + 10 = 30$

$x =$ _____

2. $80 - x = 10$

$x =$ _____

3. $x \times 8 = 24$

$x =$ _____

4. $28 \div x = 4$

$x =$ _____

5. $x + y = 15$

and $y = 5$

$x =$ _____

6. $x - y = 12$

and $y = 10$

$x =$ _____

7. $x \times y = 42$

and $y = 7$

$x =$ _____

Calculate and fill in the answers.

8. $8 + 78 + 2 =$ _____

9. $25 + 37 + 25 =$ _____

10. $80 + 59 + 20 =$ _____

11. $2 \times 8 \times 5 =$ _____

12. $2 \times 8 \times 3 =$ _____

13. $38 + 8 + 2 =$ _____

14. $78 + 9 + 1 =$ _____

15. $139 + 5 + 5 =$ _____

16. $42 \times 5 \times 2 =$ _____

17. $32 \times 5 \times 2 =$ _____

18. $3 + (^-2) =$ _____

19. $12 + (^-3) =$ _____

20. $25 + (^-10) =$ _____

21. $18 + (^-8) =$ _____

22. $5 - 7 =$ _____

23. $4 - 10 =$ _____

24. $7 - 10 =$ _____

25. $7 - 9 =$ _____

5-1   What is geometry about?

Mathematical Conversation

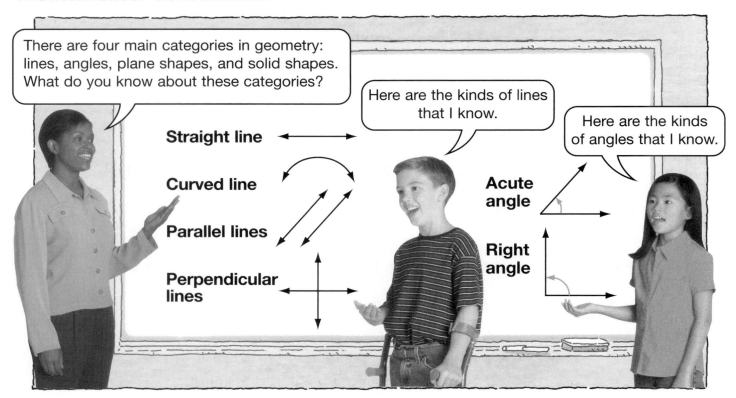

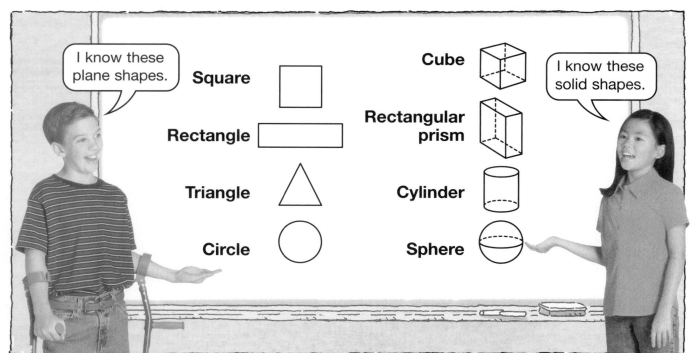

Lesson 5–1 Exercises

1. Investigate these pairs of lines. Draw a ring around the parallel lines. Draw a box around the perpendicular lines.

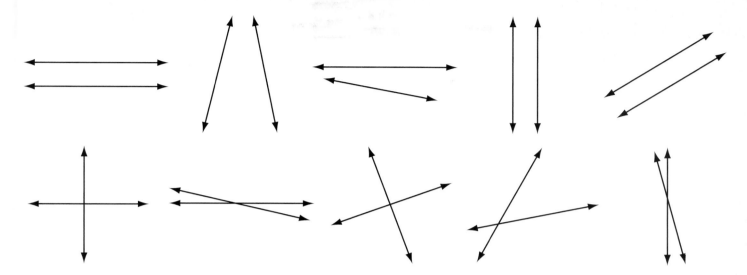

2. Investigate these shapes. Draw a ring around the plane shapes. Draw a box around the solid shapes.

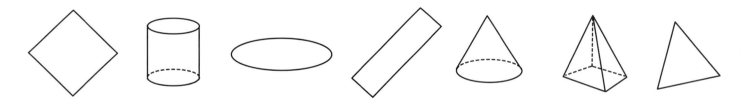

Calculate these in your mind and fill in the answers.

3. 17 + 7 = _____	**4.** 28 + 12 = _____	**5.** 79 + 3 = _____	**6.** 16 + 13 = _____
7. 9 − 5 = _____	**8.** 24 − 4 = _____	**9.** 45 − 6 = _____	**10.** 81 − 7 = _____
11. 27 + 8 = _____	**12.** 66 + 6 = _____	**13.** 86 + 5 = _____	**14.** 48 + 8 = _____
15. 32 − 12 = _____	**16.** 74 − 5 = _____	**17.** 55 − 15 = _____	**18.** 81 − 6 = _____
19. 9 × 9 = _____	**20.** 9 × 8 = _____	**21.** 9 × 7 = _____	**22.** 9 × 6 = _____
23. 45 ÷ 9 = _____	**24.** 18 ÷ 9 = _____	**25.** 27 ÷ 9 = _____	**26.** 36 ÷ 9 = _____

Reflection and Discussion

Do you know the names of any geometric shapes that were not mentioned in today's lesson?

5-2   How do we measure?

Mathematical Conversation

Units of Measurement

Inch ——

Square inch ☐

Cubic inch

Figures

1.
2.
3. ——

We use different kinds of units to measure different figures. Can you match these units of measurement with the figures they measure?

Yes, of course I can! But what about angles? How do we measure them?

I know! We use a protractor to measure angles! The smallest angle we can read is one degree.

People in other countries use the metric system. The units of length in that system are centimeters, meters, and kilometers.

I've heard that there is only one system to measure angles!

Lesson 5–2 Exercises

1. Measure these lines with a ruler and fill in the answers.

—————————————————————   _____ inches

—————————————————————————   _____ inches

———————————   _____ inches

—————————————————————————————   _____ inches

Use a ruler to draw straight lines of these lengths.

        1 inch

        6 inches

        3 inches

2. Below are two units of measurement. Draw lines connecting them with the objects they can be used to measure.

 1 inch   1 cubic inch

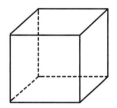   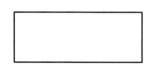   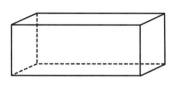

Calculate these in your mind and fill in the answers.

3. $22 + 12 =$ _____   **4.** $30 + 20 =$ _____   **5.** $55 + 11 =$ _____   **6.** $9 + 8 =$ _____

7. $15 - 5 =$ _____   **8.** $16 - 9 =$ _____   **9.** $17 - 8 =$ _____   **10.** $13 - 7 =$ _____

11. $40 + 17 =$ _____   **12.** $12 + 30 =$ _____   **13.** $34 + 10 =$ _____   **14.** $24 + 50 =$ _____

15. $22 - 11 =$ _____   **16.** $38 - 6 =$ _____   **17.** $49 - 2 =$ _____   **18.** $49 - 7 =$ _____

19. $8 \times 9 =$ _____   **20.** $8 \times 8 =$ _____   **21.** $8 \times 7 =$ _____   **22.** $8 \times 6 =$ _____

23. $40 \div 8 =$ _____   **24.** $16 \div 8 =$ _____   **25.** $32 \div 8 =$ _____   **26.** $24 \div 8 =$ _____

Reflection and Discussion   We could use an everyday object such as a pencil or a piece of string to measure our classroom. Why do we have standard units of measurement?

Warm-up Exercises

$3 \times 6 - 2 = \underline{\hspace{1cm}}$ $4 \times 7 - 8 = \underline{\hspace{1cm}}$ $8 \times 2 + 4 = \underline{\hspace{1cm}}$ $9 \times 4 - 1 = \underline{\hspace{1cm}}$

$2 + 3 \times 6 = \underline{\hspace{1cm}}$ $2 + 4 \times 7 = \underline{\hspace{1cm}}$ $10 + 8 \times 2 = \underline{\hspace{1cm}}$ $4 + 9 \times 4 = \underline{\hspace{1cm}}$

5-3   Can you make sense of polygons' names?

Mathematical Conversation

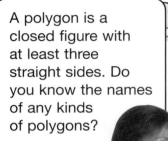

A polygon is a closed figure with at least three straight sides. Do you know the names of any kinds of polygons?

Of course! A triangle is a polygon! The prefix "tri" means "three." That is why a figure with three sides is called a triangle! Think about a tricycle with three wheels, and a tripod with three legs!

Quadrilaterals are polygons with four sides. A rectangle is a quadrilateral, and so is a square. "Quad" means "four."

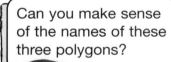

Can you make sense of the names of these three polygons?

Pentagon

Hexagon

"Penta" means "five." That is why a figure with five sides is called a pentagon.

"Hex" means "six." That's why a figure with six sides is called a hexagon.

Octagon

"Oct" means "eight." That is why a figure with eight sides is called an octagon. Think about an octopus!

Lesson 5–3 Exercises

Draw these polygons in the space provided.

1. Triangle	2. Pentagon	3. Hexagon	4. Octagon
5. Quadrilateral	6. Quadrilateral	7. Quadrilateral	8. Quadrilateral

Investigate these shapes. Write the letter of each shape in the blank next to the correct polygon name.

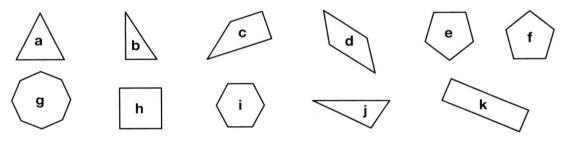

8. Triangle _____   9. Quadrilateral _____

10. Pentagon _____   11. Hexagon _____   12. Octagon _____

Calculate these in your mind and fill in the answers.

13. $13 + 13 =$ ____   14. $18 + 2 =$ ____   15. $24 + 24 =$ ____   16. $22 + 22 =$ ____

17. $12 - 6 =$ ____   18. $12 - 7 =$ ____   19. $12 - 8 =$ ____   20. $12 - 9 =$ ____

Reflection and Discussion   Draw a quadrilateral that is different from those in the lesson.

5-4   Types of angles and triangles . . .

Mathematical Conversation

Right angle   **Straight angle**   **Acute angle**   **Obtuse angle**   **Reflex angle**

- A *right angle* is 90°.
- A *straight angle* is 180°.
- An *acute angle* is more than 0° and less than 90°.
- An *obtuse angle* is more than 90° and less than 180°.
- A *reflex angle* is more than 180° and less than 360°.

> I thought angles were just angles. I never knew there were so many types!

> I didn't either. But some of these names sound weird to me!

> We can also classify triangles according to the lengths of their sides.

> We can use angles to classify triangles.

CLASSIFYING TRIANGLES ACCORDING TO THEIR ANGLES

Acute triangle   **Obtuse triangle**

Right triangle   **Equiangular triangle**

- An *acute triangle* has three acute angles.
- An *obtuse triangle* has one obtuse angle.
- A *right triangle* has one right angle.
- An *equiangular triangle* has three angles equal in measure.

CLASSIFYING TRIANGLES ACCORDING TO THEIR SIDES

Equilateral triangle   **Isosceles triangle**   **Scalene triangle**

- An *equilateral triangle* has three sides equal in length.
- An *isosceles triangle* has two sides equal in length.
- A *scalene triangle* has no sides of equal length.

Lesson 5–4 Exercises

Investigate the angles in these triangles. Write the letter of each triangle in the blank next to its name. Look carefully. Some may have more than one name.

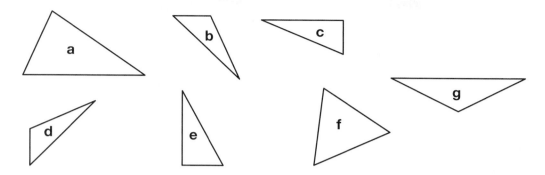

1. Acute triangle _____
2. Obtuse triangle _____
3. Right triangle _____
4. Equiangular triangle _____

Investigate the sides of these triangles. Write the letter of each triangle in the blank next to its name.

5. Equilateral triangle _____

6. Isosceles triangle _____

7. Scalene triangle _____

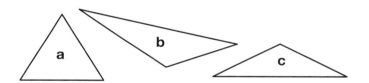

Calculate these in your mind and fill in the answers.

8. 40 + 40 = ____   9. 30 + 40 = ____   10. 20 + 30 = ____   11. 40 + 50 = ____

12. 90 − 20 = ____   13. 90 − 70 = ____   14. 80 − 50 = ____   15. 80 − 30 = ____

16. 15 + 15 = ____   17. 32 + 32 = ____   18. 23 + 23 = ____   19. 41 + 41 = ____

20. 18 − 9 = ____   21. 16 − 7 = ____   22. 14 − 6 = ____   23. 14 − 5 = ____

24. 6 × 6 = ____   25. 6 × 7 = ____   26. 6 × 8 = ____   27. 6 × 9 = ____

28. 30 ÷ 6 = ____   29. 24 ÷ 6 = ____   30. 18 ÷ 6 = ____   31. 12 ÷ 6 = ____

Reflection and Discussion

Name at least three objects in your everyday life that are shaped like triangles.

93

Draw the figure named in each box.

Lines and Angles

1. Straight line	2. Curved line	3. Parallel lines	4. Perpendicular lines
5. Right angle	6. Straight angle	7. Acute angle	8. Obtuse angle

Triangles

9. Acute triangle	10. Obtuse triangle	11. Right triangle	12. Isosceles triangle

Quiz 6

Plane Shapes

13. Square	14. Rectangle	15. Circle
16. Pentagon	17. Hexagon	18. Octagon

Solid Shapes

19. Cube	20. Rectangular prism	21. Cylinder	22. Sphere

Use a ruler to draw straight lines of these lengths.

23. 2 inches

24. 4 inches

25. 5 inches

5-6   How many types of quadrilaterals?

Mathematical Conversation

Triangles are closed figures with 3 sides; quadrilaterals are closed figures with 4 sides; pentagons . . .

Speaking of quadrilaterals, how many types do you know?

I know two: rectangles and squares!

Rectangle

Square

Rectangles and squares are similar in the sense that they all have four right angles. Have you noticed what makes them different?

It is the lengths of their sides! A rectangle has two longer sides, but a square has four sides of the same length.

I guess that is why we call the long sides of a rectangle "length," and the shorter sides "width." All the sides of a square are the same, so we just call them all "side"!

Here are some other quadrilaterals. Can you tell me how they are different from rectangles and squares?

MORE QUADRILATERALS

Parallelogram   Rhombus   Trapezoid

Lesson 5–6 Exercises

Draw these quadrilaterals in the space provided below.

1. Rectangle	2. Square	3. Parallelogram	4. Rhombus	5. Trapezoid

Investigate these quadrilaterals. Write the letter of each shape in the blank next to its name. Some shapes have more than one name.

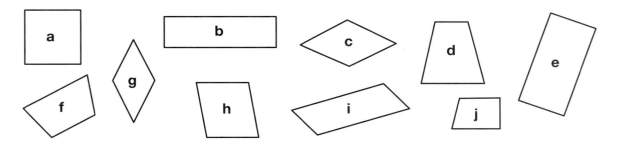

6. Rectangle _____   **7.** Square _____

8. Parallelogram _____   **9.** Rhombus _____   **10.** Trapezoid _____

Calculate these in your mind and fill in the answers.

11. $6 + 7 =$ _____   **12.** $5 + 8 =$ _____   **13.** $9 + 4 =$ _____   **14.** $4 + 7 =$ _____

15. $13 - 7 =$ _____   **16.** $14 - 6 =$ _____   **17.** $16 - 7 =$ _____   **18.** $13 - 5 =$ _____

19. $5 + 7 =$ _____   **20.** $6 + 8 =$ _____   **21.** $7 + 5 =$ _____   **22.** $8 + 6 =$ _____

23. $17 - 9 =$ _____   **24.** $11 - 6 =$ _____   **25.** $13 - 8 =$ _____   **26.** $12 - 4 =$ _____

27. $5 \times 9 =$ _____   **28.** $5 \times 8 =$ _____   **29.** $5 \times 7 =$ _____   **30.** $5 \times 6 =$ _____

31. $25 \div 5 =$ _____   **32.** $20 \div 5 =$ _____   **33.** $15 \div 5 =$ _____   **34.** $10 \div 5 =$ _____

Reflection and Discussion

Is it possible to make a rectangle or square using two right triangles of the same size and shape? Explain.

5-7   What is a circle?

Mathematical Conversation

One plane shape is very different from the shapes we've already discussed. It has no sides. It is a simple closed curve. Do you know what it is?

I think you are talking about a circle.

Yes, I agree! It is a circle!

Although circles look simple, there are important facts about them that we need to learn.

- A straight line from the center of a circle (*O*) to the curve is called the **radius**.

- A straight line through the center from one side of the circle to the other is called the **diameter**.

- The length of the curve, or the distance around the circle, is called the **circumference**.

Radius, diameter, and **circumference** are the three most important elements of a circle.

circumference

radius

diameter

O

It looks to me as if the diameter is twice as long as the radius.

The circumference is definitely the longest.

I agree with Lily.

Lesson 5-7 Exercises

1. Do you agree with these statements?

- **The circumference of a circle is about 3 times as long as its diameter.**

- **The diameter is 2 times as long as the radius.**

Now try it. Use a ruler to measure the radius and diameter of each circle, and use a string and a ruler to find their circumferences.

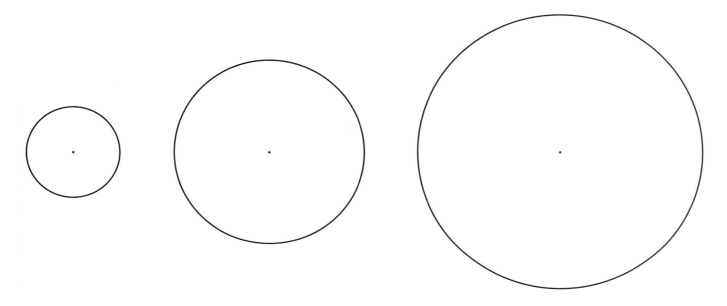

Calculate these in your mind and fill in the answers.

2. $18 + 7 =$ _____   3. $15 + 9 =$ _____   4. $13 + 8 =$ _____   5. $17 + 5 =$ _____

6. $25 - 8 =$ _____   7. $26 - 7 =$ _____   8. $22 - 9 =$ _____   9. $24 - 8 =$ _____

10. $24 + 8 =$ _____   11. $23 + 7 =$ _____   12. $26 + 5 =$ _____   13. $28 + 7 =$ _____

14. $30 - 9 =$ _____   15. $33 - 6 =$ _____   16. $35 - 8 =$ _____   17. $31 - 7 =$ _____

18. $4 \times 9 =$ _____   19. $4 \times 7 =$ _____   20. $4 \times 8 =$ _____   21. $4 \times 6 =$ _____

22. $240 \div 4 =$ _____   23. $160 \div 4 =$ _____   24. $120 \div 4 =$ _____   25. $80 \div 4 =$ _____

Reflection and Discussion

How many radii do you think you can draw in a given circle? How many diameters?

5-8   What shapes can stand up?

Mathematical Conversation

100

Lesson 5–8 Exercises

Draw the solid shapes in the boxes provided below.

1. Cube	2. Rectangular prism	3. Cylinder	4. Cone	5. Pyramid

Investigate these solids. Write the letter of each solid in the blank next to its name. Some solids may have more than one name.

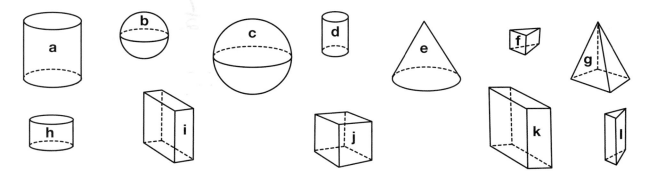

6. Rectangular prism _____   **7.** Cube _____   **8.** Triangular prism _____

9. Cylinder _____   **10.** Cone _____   **11.** Pyramid _____   **12.** Sphere _____

Calculate these in your mind and fill in the answers.

13. $13 + 21 =$ _____   **14.** $62 + 12 =$ _____   **15.** $43 + 25 =$ _____   **16.** $2 + 32 =$ _____

17. $25 - 10 =$ _____   **18.** $26 - 12 =$ _____   **19.** $44 - 14 =$ _____   **20.** $57 - 17 =$ _____

21. $24 + 42 =$ _____   **22.** $23 + 32 =$ _____   **23.** $16 + 61 =$ _____   **24.** $13 + 31 =$ _____

25. $99 - 22 =$ _____   **26.** $88 - 33 =$ _____   **27.** $55 - 44 =$ _____   **28.** $66 - 11 =$ _____

29. $3 \times 9 =$ _____   **30.** $3 \times 7 =$ _____   **31.** $3 \times 8 =$ _____   **32.** $3 \times 6 =$ _____

33. $150 \div 3 =$ _____   **34.** $120 \div 3 =$ _____   **35.** $90 \div 3 =$ _____   **36.** $60 \div 3 =$ _____

Reflection and Discussion   Draw a pentagonal solid.

101

5-9 Unit 5 Review

Mathematical Conversation

Here are the five kinds of quadrilaterals that we have learned about in this unit. If I ask you to take away the one that is least similar to the others, which would it be?

I would take away the trapezoid. In all the other figures, every pair of opposite sides is parallel. Trapezoids have only one pair of parallel sides.

In fact, in the other four figures, the opposite sides aren't just parallel. They are congruent, too. Look, the opposite angles in these figures are congruent as well.

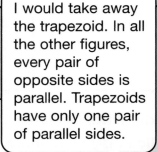

Rectangle   **Square**

Parallelogram   **Rhombus**   **Trapezoid**

If these figures are so much alike, what makes them different from each other?

Write "yes" or "no" in each box in the chart and you will find out, Lily.

The table helps a lot!

	Rectangle	Square	Parallelogram	Rhombus
Opposite sides are parallel				
Opposite sides are congruent				
Opposite angles are congruent				
All angles are congruent				
All sides are congruent				
All angles are right angles				

Lesson 5–9 Exercises

Draw these figures in the boxes provided below.

1. Straight line	2. Curved line	3. Parallel lines	4. Perpendicular lines	5. Circle
6. Right angle	7. Acute angle	8. Obtuse angle	9. Right triangle	10. Isosceles triangle
11. Rectangle	12. Square	13. Parallelogram	14. Rhombus	15. Trapezoid
16. Pentagon	17. Hexagon	18. Octagon	19. Cube	20. Sphere
21. Rectangular prism	22. Triangular prism	23. Cylinder	24. Cone	25. Pyramid

Reflection and Discussion

Is this figure a trapezoid? Explain.

6-1   Why is there only half of a car?

Mathematical Conversation

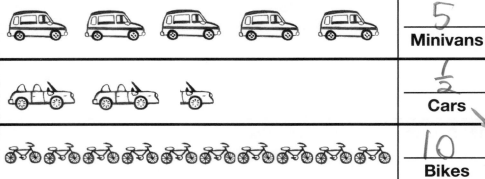

This pictograph shows the kinds and the number of vehicles that belong to the families of students in our class. Each drawing stands for 4 vehicles. Can you tell how many vehicles of each kind there are?

	5 **Minivans**
	½ **Cars**
	10 **Bikes**

Hey, Ana, you forgot to complete the last car! It only has a front half.

Ana told me that she did that on purpose. Do you know why?

I bet the number of cars is not a multiple of 4. Maybe half a car stands for 2—half of 4.

Oh! I bet it does!

Guided Practice

Calculate and fill in the answer.

If each drawing stands for 10 bicycles, how many bicycles does this pictograph stand for? _____9_____

🚲 🚲 🚲 🚲 🚲 🚲 🚲 🚲 🚲

104

Lesson 6–1 Exercises

1. Choose three kinds of writing tools such as ballpoint pens, markers, and pencils. Make a pictograph showing how many of each kind you have. Each drawing in your pictograph should stand for at least two writing tools.

- Collect the data.
- Draw the graph.
- Plan the graph.
- Label the graph (title, writing tool type, key).

_____

_____

2. As a group, count the different kinds of writing tools that you and your classmates own. Then make a pictograph of the information on the blank graph below for three of them. Each drawing in your pictograph should stand for at least four writing tools.

- Collect the data.
- Draw the graph.
- Plan the graph.
- Label the graph (title, writing tool type, key).

_____

_____

Reflection and Discussion

What ways besides pictographs could we use to show the numbers and kinds of things?

6-2   Do you agree with C.J.?

Mathematical Conversation

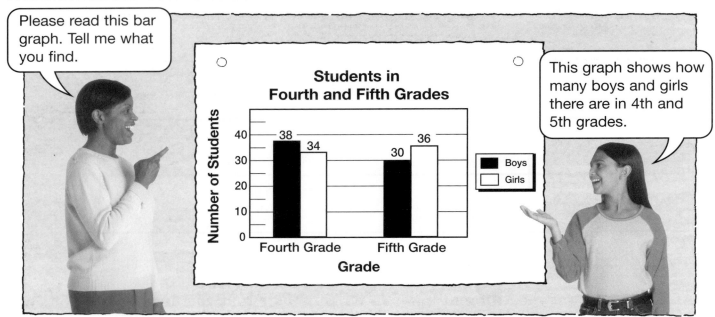

Please read this bar graph. Tell me what you find.

This graph shows how many boys and girls there are in 4th and 5th grades.

Students in Fourth and Fifth Grades

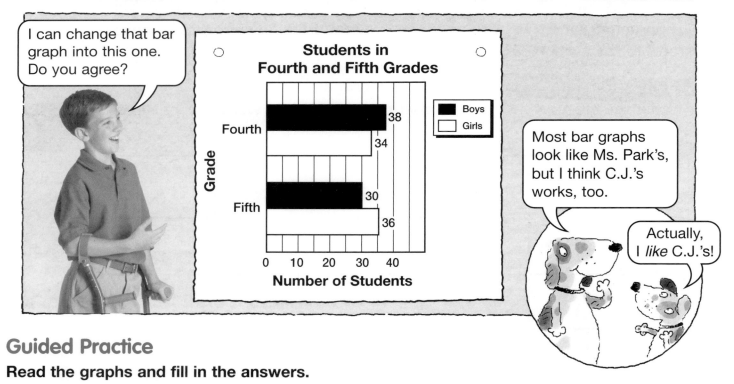

I can change that bar graph into this one. Do you agree?

Students in Fourth and Fifth Grades

Most bar graphs look like Ms. Park's, but I think C.J.'s works, too.

Actually, I *like* C.J.'s!

Guided Practice

Read the graphs and fill in the answers.

According to these graphs, the total number of girls in fourth and fifth grades is _____ and the total number of boys in fourth and fifth grades is _____.

Lesson 6–2 Exercises

For each problem: collect the data, plan the graph, draw the graph, and label the graph.

1. When he was younger, C.J. went to a very small preschool. There were 12 girls and 15 boys altogether.

   A. Make a bar graph to show the number of boys and girls in C.J.'s preschool.

   B. Make a pictograph to show the number of boys and girls in C.J.'s preschool.

2. Find out how many girls and boys there are in the third and fourth grades of your school. Then make a bar graph to show your findings.

Reflection and Discussion There were more boys than girls in C.J.'s preschool. Can you tell how many more from the bar graph? From the pictograph?

6-3   What do "up" and "down" mean?

Mathematical Conversation

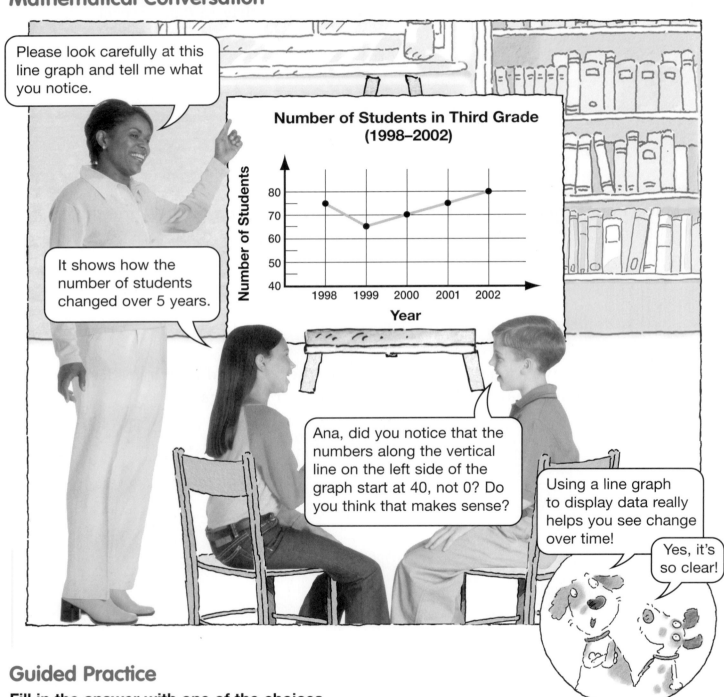

Guided Practice

Fill in the answer with one of the choices.

According to the line graph, the number of third-grade students is going _____ (down, up, or not changing).

Lesson 6–3 Exercises

For each problem: collect the data, plan the graph, draw the graph, and label the graph.

1. On the grid provided, make and label a bar graph to show the information from Ms. Park's line graph.

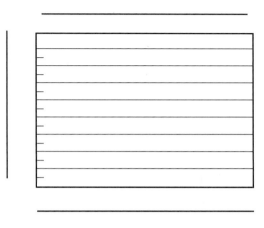

    A. There were 70 third-grade students in 2000. How many more third-grade students were there in 2001? _____

    B. How many more third-grade students were there in 2002 than in 2000?

    _____

2. Find out how many students attended your school each year for the past five years. On the grid provided, make a line graph to show your findings.

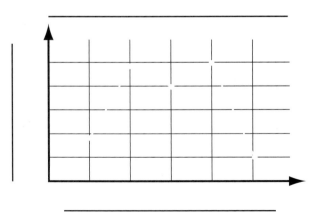

Reflection and Discussion

Why did Ms. Park use a bar graph in the last lesson, but a line graph in this lesson?

6-4   Do you like circle graphs?

Mathematical Conversation

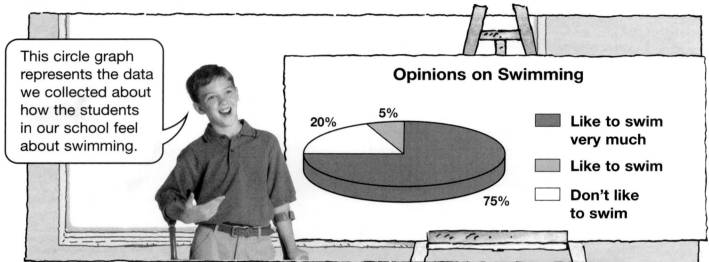

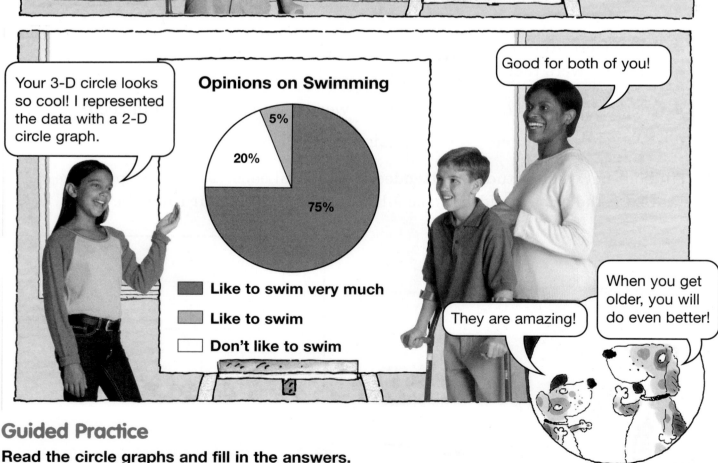

Guided Practice

Read the circle graphs and fill in the answers.

There are 100 students in C.J.'s school, so _____ students like to swim very much, _____ students like to swim, and _____ don't like to swim at all.

Lesson 6–4 Exercises

1. In Ana's school, 60% of the girls like to dance very much, 25% of the girls like to dance, and 15% of the girls don't like to dance.

Use the circle graph below to show this information. Remember to make a key.

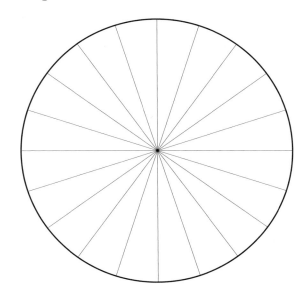

2. Last week, 40% of the students in Ana's school read more than 3 books, 30% read 3 books, 15% read 2 books, 10% read 1 book, and 5% didn't read any books.

Use the circle graph below to show this information. Remember to make a key.

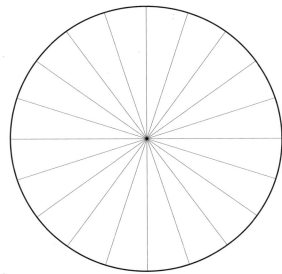

Reflection and Discussion   In each graph above, what does the whole circle represent?

Notes